a letter from the founder

J.K. Rowling observed, "No story lives unless someone wants to listen." Echoing this notion, and mindful of its begetter's struggles to be discovered, Pubslush was established principally as an opportunity for authors from all walks of life to bring their books to life, and publish successfully. The publishing lovechild of American Idol and TOMS Shoes, Pubslush is an inventive platform, democratizing publishing, marrying instinct with insight, and giving back to (aspiring) readers.

The debut novel from Pubslush Press, *a beautiful mess*, is the material embodiment of that vision. A book chosen by everyday readers, plucked from the conventionally negative slush pile, as it were. Disrupting the industry, Pubslush reinvents the slush pile positively for a new generation of involved readers. Ali Berlinski's compelling compilation of short essays could not be more ideally suited to the mission of Pubslush. Her story is endearing, witty, and speaks candidly to the young and young at heart – a fresh, honest voice that effortlessly grapples with the struggles and triumphs of this capricious life. Though perhaps the most defining moments of *a beautiful mess* are those of Ali's shrewd innocence, both charming and disconcerting in brilliant juxtaposition.

I'm confident *a beautiful mess* will become a shining beacon of hope for aspiring authors everywhere, a symbol of opportunity and philanthropy. This book not only represents a paradigm shift in a démodé industry, but will make a tangible difference in the lives of children worldwide without access to literature. The publishing revolution is here. You're holding it.

Jesse Potash
Founder, Pubslush

a beautiful mess

ali berlinski

PUBSLUSH PRESS
NEW YORK

a beautiful mess
Ali Berlinski

First published in the United States by Pubslush Press in 2013

ISBN-13: 978-0-9886028-0-9
ISBN-10: 0-9886028-0-6

Library of Congress Control Number: 2012922085

Printed in the United States of America

1 3 5 7 9 10 8 6 4 2

Pubslush Press
New York, NY

www.pubslush.com | hello@pubslush.com

flying kites

For every copy sold of *a beautiful mess*, a children's book (or its value) will be donated to Flying Kites, an orphanage and school in Njabini, Kenya.

The Pubslush Cause: To impact education initiatives by providing books, relevant resources, and logistical support to children worldwide. Through local partnerships, Pubslush will positively affect literacy rates, thereby facilitating sustainable change to combat the vicious cycle of illiteracy and poverty. Visit pubslush.org to learn more.

About Flying Kites: At Flying Kites, we believe in children. And so, in the Aberdares Mountains of Kenya, we have built a Home and Leadership Academy for orphaned children who would otherwise have nowhere to turn. Through our emphasis on exemplary care, education, and compassion, children who have suffered the devastating effects of poverty are being empowered to change our world. Visit flyingkitesglobal.org to learn more.

For Soraya, who told me to write, and so I did.

my insides

you're not white!

Being a biracial kid can be hard. Especially when you have a name that screams *I'm white*, and a face that screams *I give manicures*. No one ever knows what to do with me, and neither do I for that matter. Deciding my race has always felt like a game of tug of war. *Are you more like Mommy or Daddy?* It's the ultimate guilt trip. Attempting to remain neutral, I tend to check "other" when filling out forms, if given the option. However, even that feels strange, because what does "other" even mean? Each of those boxes represents a face. Granted, they're stereotypes, but at least they're given a face. When you think "other," what face comes to mind? All I see is an alien.

The best is when people read my name, see my face and then give me a suspicious look as if I have stolen someone's identity. Happens more often than you'd think. I handed the man at the liquor store my ID and his reply was, "Berlinski, huh? Your husband Polish?"

"Not married."

"You don't look Polish."

"Well you didn't strike me as an asshole, but here we are." Fine, I didn't say this. Instead, I smiled bitterly and said, "Well, I am."

Since I figure I look more Asian than white, I feel my difference is broadcasted even louder when I'm with my white family. One can only imagine what people think when they see me. Probably, *one of these is not like the other.* Like a game of racial duck, duck, goose that goes, blond, blond, blond, CHINKY! From an outsider's perspective I look adopted, and this was long before Madonna and Angelina Jolie popularized collecting foreign babies.

The only other plausible explanation for my presence is that I look like the daughter of my stepmom, Julie, the other brown person in the family. Growing up, I too considered this a possibility since I looked much more like Julie than my mother. Unlike me, my mother had dark skin, the color of milk chocolate. Her cheekbones were higher, her nose pointier. The only thing my mother and I shared were small Asian eyes. Julie was much more fair-skinned and, like me, had a rounded nose. Essentially, I convinced myself into believing that my mom paid Julie to give me up at birth.

Every child, at one point or another, examines his or her birth certificate hoping to find there's been a grave mistake. In actuality, they're heir to a disgusting fortune. I remember sneaking into my mom's files and examining my birth certificate. To my disappointment, everything checked out. Julie was not my mom nor was I destined to inherit a throne.

Biological or not, Julie is my mom. She's helped raise me since I was a year old. With both my parents working, my mom hired Julie, then an illegal immigrant from the Philippines, to be my nanny. Sounds cliché, right? The only thing more cliché would be if my father left my mother for my nanny, which did or did not happen, depending on who you ask. As a child, I spent so much time with Julie that I would affectionately refer to her as Mom—until my mom overheard me. Then, it was just "Julie."

Despite not being blood-related, people will often say that Julie and I look alike. We'll be out shopping, or I'll show someone a family photo and get, "You take so much after your mom." If it's someone I know, like a boyfriend's aunt, I'll gently say, "We're not actually related." Suddenly, the air changes; I've shamed them somehow by pointing out their presumption. They don't say anything, but I know they're quietly expecting an explanation. Interestingly, when I explain my family situation, they forget they're offended and attempt to comfort me. "It's okay," they'll offer, "I have a friend with a crazy family like yours." When it comes to strangers, I'll just smile. It's not worth the effort of explaining and even though Julie and I aren't related, we Asians do kind of look the same. Plus, my stepmom is beautiful and I'd much rather look like her than my father, who resembles Bill Murray.

Most people can't tell what I am, since I don't fit neatly into their understanding of race. Though over the years, the rise of biracial children has made this burden easier to bear. I've been told I look Vietnamese, Puerto Rican, Dominican, Indian, and many others that never seemed to make sense to me. But I take these observations as compliments.

I've lost count of how many times someone has asked deviously, "So, where are you from?" I know exactly what they're getting at. Nevertheless, I'll reply, "I grew up bicoastal, in Jersey and California."

"No, but where... you know, where?"

"Sacramento. It's up north."

"I mean, where are your parents from?"

I'll smile coyly and say, "My mom is from California; my dad's from Jersey."

"But originally?"

"Yeah, I get it... My mom is Filipino and my dad is Polish."

Surprisingly, it's never the Polish part that gets them; rather, it's learning I'm Filipino. "That's it! I could tell you were some type of Asian, I just couldn't figure out what. Vietnamese maybe, but I wasn't sure." Finally my olive skin, almond eyes and rounded nose all makes sense.

Playing Twenty Questions with random strangers is even worse abroad, where people's understanding of American is that we're all White and Blond. Once, while having a drink in Monaco, my girlfriends and I were approached by an older, overweight, and—judging by his brazen chest hair—overly confident man. Predictably, the first thing he asked was, "So, where are you from?"

"New York," I answered.

"I used to live there. Jes, I know New Jork very well," he said in a thick nondescript accent.

"Oh yeah, where?"

"All over. I know everywhere... Houston Street," which he pronounced as if it were the city in Texas, so I knew he was full of it. Every New Yorker can identify a tourist by the way they pronounce, or rather mispronounce, Houston Street.

"Uh huh," I mocked.

"So where are jou from? Shour English is very gewd."

"I'm from New York... *originally*."

"I lived in New Jork. I detect an accent."

Really, I thought. You want to get into this with *me*? Okay.

"My mom is Filipino and my dad is Polish, but I was born and raised in the States."

The only thing he heard out of my mouth was, "Ah Jes, the Philippines! Very nice place. Shame, the women there are all so ughly. Prostitutes. But all the Filipino women outside of the Philippines, so beautiful!" he said with a wink.

Despite my heritage, I've never identified with Filipino culture. It's tough when you don't eat the food or speak the language. I'm pretty much whitewashed or a Twinkie: yellow on the outside, white on the inside. This is partially my mom's fault, for being Americanized herself. Unlike my aunts and uncles, who grew up in the Philippines, my mom was raised in San Francisco during the seventies. She doesn't have a thick accent, was never strict like other typical Filipino parents, nor did she force my siblings and I to go to Catholic mass. We didn't eat rice everyday or have a painting of The Last Supper hanging in our living room. We didn't own a karaoke machine and we never watched TFC (The Filipino Channel).

Most of my understanding of Filipino culture comes from visiting my aunt's house or going to her parties. Every time felt like I was entering a distant land, where instead of typical American dessert they ate halo-halo, shaved ice with red beans, coconut, ube (a purple yam), and condensed milk. *Liars,* I thought. This tastes nothing like a root beer float.

The older I get, the more I realize that while I may not entirely identify with Filipino culture. I'm not white either. That definitely makes a minority, just not any one in particular. Though I suppose, if you're going to be a minority it's better to have solidarity. You don't exactly see biracial babies marching on Washington these days demanding more rights. At times I feel like I'm crying over spilt milk. Yeah, it sucks to be marginalized, but mixed people are hot. Not to mention that we have amazing genetics. I hardly ever get sick and when I do, I'm still hot.

Choosing whether I am Polish or Filipino is a day-to-day, moment–by-moment decision. Over time I've come to recognize the patterns that influence how I identify myself. Normally I don't think about what I am until I have to explain it to other people. If a person assumes I am Asian, I'll make it a point to tell them I'm mixed, adding, "with Polish." However, should they make a comment about Filipinos, suddenly I become an ambassador. Although I have no idea what the hell I'm talking about, my personal views somehow become the opinion of all Filipinos. We do not support global warming. We are accepting of gay culture. We have had several female presidents.

Deciding my race wouldn't be an issue if it didn't involve a hierarchy. In terms of privilege, there is nothing higher or even equal to being white. You'd think being half-white would give me some advantage over those who are fully ethnic, but it doesn't seem to work that way. In actuality, it reasserts my non-whiteness. Whereas the "one-drop rule" automatically qualifies you as black, having one drop of minority disqualifies you from being white. It's not that I want to be white; I just find the criteria amusing. The Polish aren't exactly known as the master race. We make great pierogies and kielbasa; but mostly I'd say the Polish are just another poor working class. All the same, it's a club I can't be a member of, nor do I want to. There's something gratifying about being biracial and a minority.

Having minority status gives you the ability to say things like, "Filipinos are the blacks of Asia." My mom said that once, and I stared at her. Did she really just say that? Then she added, "We can dance, sing, and play basketball!"

Everyone knows it's not racist when a minority says it. Conceivably, this is the same entitled feeling my white father must get when he declares, "I'm not prejudiced; I have a Filipino daughter and wife, for crying out loud!"

That's the danger of polarizing the word "racist." It's so taboo that no one thinks they are racist, and yet everyone has done or thought something racist at some time or another. You do the math.

Most people don't know when they're being racist. The first time I went to Madrid, a man at a bar—a friend of a friend—pulled his eyes back and pointed at me, laughing. I've been told that in Spain, it's not considered offensive, but rather a benign observation. He was merely pointing out that my eyes are squinty. In the U.S. it would be like twirling your finger to describe someone with curly hair. People might look at you funny for stating the blatantly obvious, but it certainly wouldn't offend them.

Now that I live in Spain, I've discovered that here it is completely fine to call someone a "chino" or "oriental." The concept of political correctness and racial discrimination is foreign to this culture. Dollar stores are called Chinos; my favorite is my local Super Chino. From a casual glance, it might appear that the Spanish are racists. Standing there in the bar, watching a grown man slant his eyes at me, I would've agreed. However, the lack of diversity here makes any person of difference not just an oddity, but also an exciting advent. Prejudices do exist, yet their actions generally come from ignorance, and as time goes by I try to remind myself of this. A few days later, the guy from the bar requested to be my friend on Facebook. He can't be prejudiced; we're friends!

Before moving to Spain, I had to obtain a letter of good conduct at a precinct in lower Manhattan. When my turn came, I walked up to the woman in charge of the letters, sitting in a rolly chair that appeared to conform to the exact intricacies of her body. I imagined her sitting in this chair day after day for thirty years, taking slip after slip of paper, only to enter it mindlessly into the computer. Without turning around to look at me, she stuck up her hand and wiggled her fingers, motioning for my papers.

I stood behind her, watching her key in my information. Everything seemed routine until she got to the bottom of the form. There, I noticed a piece of information that was not listed on my form—race—under which she checked "white." I could only assume it was my name, as nothing about Alison Berlinski screams minority or mixed race.

I wondered if I should say something.

With her back still turned to me she asked, "Everything correct?" Unsure what to do, I said, "Yeeaaah," stretching out every sound out in an uneasy tone.

Finally, she turned around, took one look at me, and exclaimed, "You're not white! What are you?"

Judging by her tone, she was not concerned about insulting me. I, on the other hand, was shocked and slightly offended. I'm not sure what bothered me more—her assumption that I was white or her assumption that I wasn't.

My initial reaction was to cry in horror, "What do you mean I'm not white? What will I tell my mother?" But that was too dramatic. My second option was to thank her, as if the information was like a piece of lettuce stuck between my teeth: "Oh, you're right! I'm not white! Thank you. Why didn't anyone tell me sooner?" Or I could've reprimanded her. "What are you talking about? Of course I'm white!" Then she'd feel confused and ashamed. How dare she talk to a white woman this way? She'd beg me not to get her fired. Then I, the benevolent white woman, would spare her by accepting her pitiful apology.

Despite my better judgment, I decided not to fuck with her. This was her job and she was only trying to clear up what she considered a mistake. I shook my head and said, "You can just put 'Other,'" pretending we'd reached some sort of compromise.

grab-a-bite

At four I started kindergarten and like most children, I hated it. I hated being away from my mom. I can remember banging my fists against the window each morning, crying and begging her to take me with her as I watched her leave for work. I didn't want to go to school. The other kids made me feel anxious. I wasn't teased or an outcast; all the same, I never felt like I fit in. Having skipped preschool, I didn't know any nursery songs. Thus, when it came time to sing in class, I sat there paralyzed, staring at my classmates in bewilderment. What are you doing, I thought. Whatever it was, I wanted no part of it.

I had one friend, Brandy, and even she didn't like me that much. Our mothers forced us into friendship. They were the only two Filipino women on the block, so naturally their daughters had to become friends. Were Brandy a nice person, this would have worked out just fine. However, most of our friendship consisted of her calling me fat and dumb, probably because I didn't know those stupid nursery rhymes.

Worst of all was my teacher, whom I found to be condescending. My parents didn't believe in baby talk or coddling. "Rots the mind," they'd say. Instead, they talked to me as they would any normal person, making my teacher's overenthusiastic tone and exaggerated pronunciations confusing and unbearable. She thinks I'm stupid, I thought.

I detested her idiotic and poorly worded questions that never asked what they truly meant. To protest, I often gave contrary answers to what I considered asinine questions. Every day, right before snack time, she'd play a word association game. But I was hungry, and all I could think about was my salami sandwich, calling to me from my pink Minnie Mouse lunchbox. Sometimes, my mom would cut my sandwich into a teddy bear or rocking horse with a cookie cutter and include a cute note like *love you, xoxo Mom*. The notes were nice, but I hated when she cut my sandwiches because they left me with less actual sandwich. Though I had no idea how to tell time, my eyes kept glancing at the clock, figuring this is what people do when they're impatient.

Showing the class a picture of a fireman, she asked, "What are you thinking of?" I rolled my eyes and let out a deep sigh as if I had stepped into the slow checkout aisle at a supermarket. *Speed it up*, I thought, as I listened to my classmates' cliché responses. When my turn came I knew very well what she wanted me to say something along the lines of fire, a hose, or a ladder. However, she asked what are you thinking about, not

grab-a-bite

what does this make you think of and so I told her the truth, a salami sandwich. I was hungry. I was making a point.

Judging from her look, she didn't find this funny. I quickly discovered that not everybody enjoys sarcasm, particularly from a four-year-old. When my mom got home that night we had a talk. Apparently, she didn't find it funny either. The teacher was concerned I wasn't concentrating in class and mistook my humor for deficiency. "It's because I don't know those stupid songs!" I cried. This was the end of my sarcasm in school, and the beginning of my stomachaches.

Like clockwork, every morning as I turned the corner to school, there it was: a pit in my stomach. When I complained to my mother, she asked, "How does it hurt?" How does my stomach hurt? I wasn't prepared for this question. "Is it like someone's punching you in the stomach or like you're going to throw up?" I was four and the thought of being punched in the stomach had never occurred to me. Unable to relate, I said, "Um, like vomit." With a mother's suspicious stare, she pressed her hand against my forehead. I don't have a fever; I have a stomachache! *Down here!* I wanted to point, motioning toward my stomach. Not surprisingly, she didn't find anything. Yet, after a long hesitant pause, she sighed, "All right, you can come with me to the truck," meaning that I didn't have to go to school that day. Instantly my stomach felt much better.

My mom has worked almost every job imaginable, from architect to caterer. When I was four, my mom ran a lunch

13

truck called Grab-a-bite. It served breakfast and lunch to factory workers at a plant near our house in New Jersey. Using his skills as a graphic designer, my step-dad had created the logo, a green outline of a hand grabbing the name written as if it were a sandwich. I can still see it painted across the white metal of the truck.

Nothing made me happier than being on the truck with my mom. Before I started school that fall, she would take me with her to work. It was a time for just the two of us. Plus, on the truck, I didn't feel stupid or like a child. I got to ride in the front seat, the very definition of being an adult when you're four.

The truck was old and rattly. Riding in it felt like being on an old amusement ride, in which half the experience lies within the fear that at any moment the one bolt holding everything together will finally give out. Then again, that's also half the fun. I loved everything about the truck: the way it shook, the clang of the equipment falling, and the sound of my mom laughing when we drove over a pothole. I loved the smell of the grill and the way it sizzled when my mom fried an egg. Mostly, I loved being with my mom.

Mornings were my favorite part of the day. Every morning I'd wake up and tell my mom my stomach hurt. After a few moments of suspicious staring, she'd motion for me to grab my jacket. First thing we did was drive to Dunkin' Donuts. My mom always let me get a donut for myself and at four there

was clearly only one option: a pink frosted donut with rainbow sprinkles. As she drove, I'd eat my donut, dropping sprinkles everywhere and smearing pink icing across my face. Perfect moments.

Working the truck was easy. There were only two hours when it got busy: breakfast and lunch. During these times, my mom let me take orders while she manned the grill. I enjoyed talking to the workers. I'd ask them how their day was, how they wanted their egg cooked, if they had kids my age. Then my mom said I asked too many questions and demoted me to just telling her if we had a customer. Otherwise, there was a lot of downtime, which was usually spent singing along to the radio. I loved the soothing sound of my mom's voice.

As it turned out, my stomachache lasted for two weeks. For a while, I thought I was in the clear, until school called and informed my mom I'd be held back if I missed any more days. I figured there are worse things, but my mom wouldn't hear it. I bawled all night on our living room floor, kicking and flailing my limbs, my mom sidestepping around me as she cleaned and ignored my cries. I cried until I became too dehydrated to cry anymore. Defeated, I returned to school the following Monday with my Minnie Mouse lunch box and my stomachache.

A few months later the truck's brakes failed while my mom was driving downhill, sending her flying through a red light. Thank God for the emergency brake, which she used to bring

the truck to a stop. The fiasco left my mom shaken. As for the truck, repairs were too costly; my parents were forced to put it down. Grab-a-bite was scrapped and sold.

In the end, I got what I wanted; my mom came back home. Still, we never did get back that special time together. Incidentally, the truck's death came at a perfect time; she was pregnant and soon I would have a baby sister, Monika. She was a welcomed addition to the family. I couldn't wait for my sister to come home and when she did, life changed. My grandma came to live with us and my mom stayed home to take care of Monika. Time passed, I hated school a little less, and I forgot about the truck.

It wasn't until years later, during a therapy session, that I recalled my time on the truck with my mom. "What was your first happy memory with your mom?" the therapist asked. Initially, nothing came to mind. I sat silently for what seemed like an eternity trying to remember a time when I felt close to her. It took a while, but eventually, I remembered the truck, my donut-caked face, and my mom's laughter as we drove over potholes.

role playing

While making polite conversation, people will often ask if I have siblings, to which I'll answer yes. Predictably, they'll ask how many and I feel misleading when I tell them four. "Big family," they'll remark and I can imagine what they must be picturing: a van full of Asians and me, the poster child of population control. It's true, I have a big family, but what I want to explain to them is that we didn't all grow up together nor are we all Asian.

Generally, I abhor making small talk. All the same, I can't resist an opportunity to discuss my family. The way I look at it, what's the use in having a fucked-up family if it doesn't make for interesting conversation? It's like going into a poker match with a royal flush; I'm guaranteed to have the best hand. Who else can say they are the oldest, youngest, middle and only child? I've yet to meet another person with my same situation, and if I did, I'm not sure whether I'd be excited to learn I'm not alone or if the only child in me would be upset at the prospect of sharing.

Hearing my family situation generally confuses people, as if my life were some sort of riddle that they must now somehow solve. So you're an only child with step or adopted siblings? I'll laugh and say no, the way you do to a child when they say something outrageous. Though, really, their confusion is understandable. The easiest way to describe my family situation in a way that everyone will understand, particularly my generation, is to say that it's complicated.

Explaining my family tree requires a flow chart, seven Venn diagrams, and a special iPhone app. I myself couldn't make sense of all the marriages, remarriages, and divorces, until I was at least ten. Both of my parents have been married three times. However, as my dad likes to point out, unlike my mother he's only been divorced once. After his first wife died, he married my mom, and divorced her after only one year of marriage. Fifteen years later he married again, this time to my stepmom (and former nanny) Julie, to whom he is still married to today. Are you still with me?

Of my father's three children, I am the youngest. From my father's first marriage, I have two older half-brothers, Michael and Brian, who are seven and five years older than me, respectively. Half Polish and half Italian, both of them are tall, fit, and unlike myself, clearly white. Though Michael and Brian don't exactly look alike, you wouldn't give them a raised eyebrow if they told you they were brothers. Stick me in the equation, however, and things get a little foggy. Once at

a family reunion, a distant relative I was meeting for the first time asked me if I was Michael's date. I scrunched my face in disgust. "I'm Peter's daughter, Michael's SISTER." We make an odd family portrait, though an undeniably handsome one.

After my parents divorced, my mom was awarded sole custody of me. This meant I only saw Michael and Brian every other weekend. Though our time together was limited, we easily fell into our assigned birth roles. With a B.A. from Wesleyan and a master's from MIT, Michael is your typical overachieving first child. Conversely, Brian, being the middle child, has always been an individualist.

To be fair, Brian never had to strive to be different; he just is. Personally, I love having a brother who's unique. For one, it makes me seem that much more remarkable than whomever I'm conversing with, which is really the only thing that concerns me. "Oh yeah? Well, I have a deaf brother who's also gay." I'll say it as if I had just bested them in a sporting event, the other person still generally unaware that it's a competition.

Appropriately, they'll ask, "Oh, so do you speak sign language?" to which I'll bow my head in shame, for "speaking" is a generous description of my capabilities. "Butchering" is actually what I do to the language. Although I know a few signs, mostly I speak what I like to call Ali Sign Language or ASL (formerly known as American Sign Language). Lament as I might over my inability to speak the language, their question is exactly what I expect and moreover, want them

to ask as it allows me to boast some more about my unique family.

Sadly, my infrequent visits to New Jersey, coupled with Brian's ability to read lips, made it easy for me to elude learning sign language. Not that my dad made much of an effort either. To this day, he'll sign the first letter of each word and shake it in the air as if that were the appropriate sign. Simultaneously, he'll verbally say the words, making sure to stretch the pronunciation, the way one does when they think someone doesn't speak English, "ARRRRRE YOOOOUU REEAAADDDYY?" Unable to differentiate whom he's talking to, my father will not just do this to Brian, but to all of us. My father dwells on my brother's deafness; I forget.

Although the federal government lists deafness as a disability, I've never seen my brother as disabled. It's hard to imagine how such a word could be used to describe Brian when he's completely capable of doing everything I can, if not more. Other than his hearing aids, which he stopped wearing in college, and his failure to react when I jump out from behind him and yell, "Boo!" there was never really a way to know he was deaf. Thanks to amazing teachers and speech pathologists, nothing about his voice when he speaks indicates that he can't hear. In fact, I'm not sure how I learned my brother was deaf. I can't remember anyone sitting me down to tell me there was anything different about Brian. Growing up, we were never taught to look at Brian as special so it never struck me as odd

that we watched TV with closed captioning, that Brian's alarm clock vibrated instead of rang, and that every now and again, I'd receive weird voice messages from telephone relay operators saying things like, "Hey, Ali, it's Brian just calling to say I love you!" While I don't regret disregarding my brother's deafness, I do wish I were better at sign language.

One of the great things about sign is that it's highly interpretive, and thus perfect for inside jokes. Like any other language, its subtleties allow for many comical misunderstandings. Take for instance the sign for *coffee*, which is ironically similar to *make out*. Both signs require two closed fists stacked on one another, the difference being a slight twist in the wrist for make out versus a circular motion for coffee. If I'm not careful, I'll wake my brother up and ask him if he'd like to make out. After the second time, I've just started to ask him to make out. Regrettably, he always refuses.

I told this as an anecdote at a dinner party and had a girl ask, "Then what's the sign for handjob?" She moved her hands as if she were grinding a peppermill. Everyone at the party shrieked in horror.

"I'm not sure why you're still giving handjobs, but that is definitely *not* how you give one."

"That's how you give someone an Indian burn."

"Do they like that?"

"Please stop torturing men."

Also eerily similar are the signs for *lesbian* and *lunch*. On occasion, I'll ask my brother if he's hungry for some lesbian rather than lunch. Preferring men to women, he'll decline my offer and I'll shrug my shoulders as if to say, *suit yourself, more for me!*

With statements like that it's hard to miss my traits, which shout mischievous and spoiled baby sister. Like many younger children, I quickly learned how to take advantage. Whenever Brian and I fought I'd run to Michael crying, and watch him as he chastised Brian. "You know you have to be nice to her. She's a lot younger. Play nice."

My behavior can easily be blamed on my brothers, who have never failed to indulge me. They doted on me, making me feel loved and special. At night they would tuck me into bed, only after reading and rereading *The Lorax* to me. Other nights when I couldn't sleep, Brian would come and stroke my head, softly singing excerpts from *The Sound of Music* until I fell asleep. This was long before I learned Brian was gay, what gay meant, and the stereotypes that come with being gay. Seemingly, those telltale signs you realize in retrospect didn't throw up any rainbow flags. All I knew is that this brother in particular loved playing dollhouse with me, and there was nothing strange about that.

At seven every Saturday morning, I'd promptly wake up Michael to watch my favorite show with me, *Mighty Morphin Power Rangers*. Being the obliging older brother that he is, he

would obey my demands before immediately proceeding back to bed. Brian was invited too; however, to this day, waking him up remains an impossible task. It requires a group effort and hours of hard work. We each take turns shaking him, using various ploys to get him out of bed, but to no avail. He lies there as long as he wants, and eventually we give up.

As the youngest, I looked to my older brothers to set the example. I worshiped them and naturally, their tastes became my taste. If Michael liked Nirvana, so did I. If Brian liked *Aeon Flux*, I did too. I didn't understand what any of these things were; I just assumed if my brother's were doing it, it must be cool. Consequently, I got to do all of the cool stuff at an early age, like play Dungeons and Dragons. When I got older, I was going to be in the marching band just like Michael!

Growing up, I thought they were geniuses: Michael, god of math and science, and Brian, master of the written word. In high school Brian memorized the dictionary, thereby making it futile to play any word game with him. Luckily, Brian granted me a handicap, since I was five years his junior. For instance, if we were playing Boggle, he had to find words with four or more letters whereas I could use any word I could spell. Initially, I felt a sense of accomplishment as I glanced at my list. There were so many words: *hat, ball, bash*. However, these feelings lasted only until Brian presented his, which contained words like *thorax, cranium*, or *osmosis*. Needless to say, I never came close to beating him. Eventually, I stopped trying to compete with my older brothers, whose accomplishments seemed insurmountable. Still, their successes made me wonder where I fit in. Sure, I was the pretty one and a real people person, but I wanted them to think I was smart too. I wanted them to see me as their equal.

The day I received my acceptance to NYU, I let out a sigh of relief. I thought, now I don't have to work so hard to prove my intelligence. My acceptance made my father beam with pride: his daughter, me, the brains of the family. Three months later, Michael got his acceptance from MIT grad school along with Carnegie Mellon and all the other top engineering programs. While I was happy for my brother, inside I felt a little deflated. Way to steal my thunder, bro, way to steal my thunder.

One winter when Michael was at MIT, Brian and I went to visit him. I was nineteen and excited to finally party with my older brothers. Before I arrived Michael warned me, "I'm going to take you to a party, but it may be different from the parties you're used to. People here are kind of nerds." I scoffed and told him, "I'm not stupid. I have tons of friends who are nerds. I'm a nerd! I'll be fine." It's true, I'm just as much a nerd as my brothers; however, having big boobs makes it easier to camouflage that fact.

Come the party, I spent an hour trying to duck out of a conversation with my brother's classmate, who described his thesis on worms, followed by, "So do you have a boyfriend?"

role playing

I should have known that if Michael was calling someone a nerd, it was the real deal. Never in my life have I walked into a room and known I was the coolest person there. After that party, Michael told me his friends would occasionally ask about his "cool" sister.

As much joy as I take from being a spoiled baby sister, nothing is more satisfying than being the oldest child. Most people think that being the firstborn is a burden to bear, with all the pressure to set an example, or be the bigger person. While this may be true, I chose to respond to the pressure by performing differently than most. As the firstborn of my mom's three kids, I spent most of my formative years being a mini-tyrant to my sister and brother.

Being much older and thus craftier, I became adept at the fine art of torture. Just after the release of the first and (in my opinion) best *Land Before Time*, I decided I needed a pet dinosaur. Since there were none at my disposal I resolved to take matters into my own hands and create one. I trained my younger brother and sister to sit, speak, and beg. They even had pet names: Chocolate and Plunger. Using scrunchies as collars and shoelaces as leashes, I'd walk them around the house. When asked by my mother what I was doing, I casually replied, "playing," slyly shooting her my most innocent smile.

Naturally, Kyle, being the only boy as well as the youngest, got the worst of it. When he was three and still learning to talk I told him, "You know how artists paint really well? Well, autistic people speak very well."

"I speak well... I'm autistic!"

"Yes you are!"

For the rest of the day he greeted everyone with, "Hi! I'm Kyle. I'm autistic!" This did not please my mother but it amused me for an entire day.

During high school, Kyle refused to cut his nails. At one point his toenails grew so long that I renamed them talons. After nagging and cajoling, I resorted to threats: "If you don't cut your nails I'll paint them!" The next day, when he woke up, he found his left hand was neatly manicured with hot pink nail polish. Conveniently, the nail polish remover was nowhere to be found. Ah, the good old days. We still reminisce about those times. Looking at him today, the great guy that he is, I can't help but pat myself on the back knowing I gave him character and good hygiene.

Despite growing up together, my younger siblings and I are extremely different. Half Puerto Rican and half Filipino, they look more Hispanic, and are twice my size in height and girth. Next to them I look like the baby of the family. Kyle—who I fondly call chinky beaner—often gets confused for being Mexican, since he lives in California where every remotely Hispanic-looking person is assumed to be Mexican, an immigrant, or both. Once while returning from a church mission to Mexico, he was stopped by the Border Patrol. A van full of white Christian kids and the only one asked to show his passport was, of course, my brown baby brother. "So they caught the church trying to smuggle you back in, eh?" I teased.

It reminded me of a time when I read a story about immigration to my third-grade students in Brooklyn, where I taught for three years right after college. *Immigrant* being a vocabulary word, I asked my class if they knew what the word meant. Suddenly, my groggy class woke up, their hands excitedly wiggling in the air. Before I could call on one, they cried out in unison, "Mexicans!" I covered my mouth half in shock and half to stifle my laughter.

Some family resemblances aren't inherently obvious. Then—out of the power of suggestion, close proximity, or mere observation—similarities become glaring. This is not the case with my sister and I, as our differences only seem to become more noticeable when standing next to each other. Despite being five years younger, Monika developed boobs the same time I did and has somehow always looked older. What's more, she's a good head taller and considering her build, I'm pretty sure she could bench me. Like our mother, she'll spend hours grooming herself, applying ostentatious makeup and fake eyelashes. Not me. My idea of grooming, on a good day, is brushing my hair before going out the door.

Compared to her, I'm pretty vanilla. Monika not only veers from the norm, she expresses her disdain for it. An individual and an artist, she has always used her body as a canvas. For the comic convention Comicon, she even makes her own hair. One year, she attached yellow yarn to the sides of her head like faux *Sailor Moon* pigtails. In many ways I envy her creativity. And while we're terribly different, I love her to death.

Being the oldest, I took the liberty of playing disciplinarian, which suited my bossy nature very well. Mothering came rather naturally to me, even though I made it up as I went along.

"Okay, new rule. You cannot eat more than one bowl of cereal a day," I told them, after Kyle had eaten the entire box of the good sugary cereal in just one sitting. The next day, doing as he was told, Kyle grabbed the largest bowl he could find, and filled it with the second-best cereal. "Okay, new rule…" I began, amused by my brother's ingenuity.

When rules were broken, "Go to the corner!" was my signature punishment and like good children, they always dutifully obeyed. There they'd sit, quietly and patiently, until a few hours later when I'd hear, "Can I come out now?" I only forgot them once or twice. I always felt awful afterwards, and would make amends with ice cream.

Now that they're older, I realize I can't tell them what to do anymore. For one, they don't listen when I tell them to go to the corner. More importantly, they're adults and I'm not their mother. Still, family dynamics are hard to change.

Admittedly, trying to be their cool older sister is hard. It's not unusual for sisters to confide in one another about things like their sex life. And yet, when it comes to my baby sister, suddenly I transform into Mother Teresa, preaching about how sex is a meaningful act between two married people. Or, better yet, preaching abstinence.

Even more difficult is negotiating my identity when all of my siblings come together. Should I be the bratty baby sister or the authoritarian older sibling? As it turns out, I don't have to be either. They'll spend so much time talking to one another and forgetting about me that I'm suddenly stuck in the role of the middle child and filled with a desperate need for attention. With two older siblings and two younger siblings who are symmetrically five and seven years apart from me, that's exactly what I am—the middle child. Perhaps I would be better at coping with these situations had they occurred more frequently while I was growing up. However, my two sets of siblings have only met twice.

The first time all my siblings came together was for my sixteenth birthday. That year I was scheduled to spend Christmas and my birthday in Sacramento with my mom, her new boyfriend, and my two younger siblings. As a surprise, Michael and Brian flew out from New Jersey during their college winter break. When they arrived, it was clear that their presence confused Monika and Kyle, who still didn't understand their relationship to my older brothers. Over the years they had come to hear stories of Michael and Brian, and watched as I bounced between the two coasts and consequently, two families. However, until that point both my families had yet to meet or interact.

Though all of my siblings are only half to me, they are "whole" to one another. Nevertheless, none of us were ever raised to see a difference. Hence my surprise when at one point Monika asked Michael, "Since Ali's our half sister, and you're her half brother, does that make you our quarter sibling?" Michael laughed and explained it didn't work that way. Though you've got to admit, that was not a bad deduction for a nine-year-old.

With the exception of Brian almost cutting his ear off in a freak skiing accident, thereby earning him the nickname Van Gogh, our week together was a complete success. Whole, half, quarter or not, everyone got along fabulously. Using the same handicap rule given to me as a child, Monika accomplished what I had previously deemed impossible: she beat Brian at Boggle. No one was more impressed than Brian.

As happy as I was to finally have all my siblings together, it made me realize what I'd been missing all those years. Completeness. For despite having four siblings and two families, I've always felt somewhat like an only child, lonely and alone. As a result, I've never seen myself as part of a family but rather, a book on loan. I don't belong to anyone and my time with everyone is always just temporary.

take two

One of the secret perks that come with being a child of divorce that people rarely talk about is that you get two of everything: two Christmases, two birthdays, two Easter baskets. You name it; I had two. Then there are the guilt presents, things you get as compensation for not providing a healthy upbringing. When I was four, my father bought me a handmade wooden dollhouse. It wasn't because I asked for one; rather, he felt I needed one. Guilt. It's hard to feel upset about your parents getting divorced when it translates into more presents. As far as this four-year-old was concerned, divorce was a gold mine.

I never understood why everyone got so upset about divorce; for me, it was always something normal. Divorce is all I've ever known. Before I could fully talk (mind you, I'm a fast learner), my parents divorced. Consequently, I have never known my parents as a couple. Imagining them together only confused me. *Why would you ever marry him, or vice versa?* One would be hard-pressed to find two more incompatible people. Without this idea of what life was like before, I was robbed of having a "divorced kid" complex. There was no need to see a therapist, act out, or harbor resentment toward one, or both of my parents. In spite of my parents' divorce, I was a happy child.

By the time I was three, my mother remarried. Juan and my mother met at a wedding. He was a few years younger than my mother and like many others in the eighties he had a Jheri curl mullet. Though he was Puerto Rican, people would always come up to him and speak Greek or Italian, since he had one of those faces that could easily blend in anywhere.

Still too young to understand what remarrying meant, I happily welcomed my stepfather. The man spoiled me rotten, and really, what more does a three-year-old need to know when making a character judgment? Sadly, this meant forfeiting my divorced-kid crown once again. Never was I to yell, "You're not my father!" before angrily storming to my room. Juan has never been anything but a wonderful father to me, and has always treated me as his own.

With a stepfather in the picture and a baby sister on the way, I managed to avoid the curse of being the child of a single mother. It may not have been the typical nuclear family; even so, it had all the necessary components—a mother, a father, and two-point-five children. The only thing missing was a dog, and we eventually got a rescued terrier named Bobo. Indeed, in them, I had everything a young girl could want or need. Yes, I was immune to the effects of divorce; they should do studies on me. Or so I thought.

However, leading a double life became much more complicated upon turning nine, when my mom decided that we (her, my stepfather, my new baby siblings, dog and I) were moving to California. With distance, the guilt gifts dwindled. Not that it mattered; I wasn't a child anymore whose emotions could be assuaged with a Teddy Ruxpin. Suddenly, divorce was not so fun. Divorce became less about what I got and more about what I lost—time.

That year I began flying cross-country alone. One month out of every summer and every other Christmas, I got to see my father and brothers in New Jersey. Shortly after I started traveling, I began telling my friends I was the newest member of the Mile High Club, thinking the phrase referred to how high the plane was from the ground. Really, my intention was to tell my friends that I fly a lot. In fact, I flew so much as a child that to this day, I feel a tinge of nostalgia whenever stepping into an airport. One might say I am somewhat of an airport connoisseur.

Before the age of thirteen, I had seen the airport of almost every major city: Atlanta, Chicago, Minneapolis, Los Angeles, San Francisco, Houston, Phoenix, and even Las Vegas. I had even created my own airport rating system, which evaluated airports using a five-point system based on food, seating, and general aesthetic. Phoenix was always at the top of my list, purely on the basis that from the terminal you can see Camelback Mountain, appropriately named since it looks like a sleeping camel. What choice did I have but to give it a full five points for aesthetics? None of the other airports stood a chance.

The flying didn't bother me, nor did the airports. If anything, it was what flying represented: the separation of my two worlds. Though they have always been divided, never before had I such a clear physical reminder of the fact. Every time I boarded a flight, ate airplane food, and waited for my luggage, I remembered. Flying meant leaving. I was always flying and so I was always leaving. Subsequently, time with family felt bittersweet, realizing that if I'm here, I'm not there. Eventually, the physical distance fostered mental distance. Regardless of where I was, my mind was elsewhere, wondering what my loved ones were doing on the other side of the country. Effectually, no matter where I was, it was away.

Without my brothers, my only companions at my father's house were boredom and loneliness. There weren't any kids in the neighborhood who were my age and so I had to devise ways to entertain myself with these things called books. Otherwise, most of my time was spent with my face pressed against the windows, searching for signs of life under the age of sixty. My father didn't count. He's never been much of a talker except for when it comes to food. And for a child, that's an acquired taste.

Then again, there was Julie. Explaining her role in the family has always been, well, difficult. "So she's your dad's girlfriend," my best friend Soraya said. "God no!" I snapped. They slept in separate rooms, in separate parts of the house. They never showed affection. It wasn't like that. Julie was just—Julie. There was no other way to describe it.

Actually, Julie started out as my nanny. I was only a year old when she came to us and by then I had already gone through several nannies: Sonia from Poland, who let me run around naked until the neighbors complained; Rashida from Jamaica who literally thought New York's streets were paved with gold; and more whose names and stories I've never been told or can't remember. Like many immigrants when they first come to America, Julie found herself alone in a foreign place. Hoping to help out a fellow Filipina, my mother hired her. Shortly thereafter, my parents filed for separation.

Rather than come with my mom and I, Julie stayed with my dad, helping to take care of my two older brothers until they were old enough to take care of themselves. When that day came, Julie went back to school and became a nurse—the American dream for a Filipina. Julie had been with us for so long that my brothers and I just came to accept her as family. She lives in our house. She comes to all our family events. She even vacations with my dad, but like I said, it's not romantic or weird. They're friends, just friends.

This is what I told people, until I turned sixteen and my dad proposed to Julie. No one was more shocked than my brothers and I. None of us knew they were dating, and judging by Julie's face, I'm not sure she knew either. She accepted, of course, because they'd both be lost without one another. A year later, they were married. Afterwards, explaining Julie to people became much easier, though little about their relationship changed.

Never content with where I was, I'd return to California and long to be back with my brothers in New Jersey, forgetting of course about my friends—boredom and loneliness. Moreover, whenever someone in California asked where I was from, I'd reply, "Jersey." At the time, I thought it made me unique and exotic. None of my other classmates had been to the East Coast. They were all born and raised in Sacramento. How boring, I thought. When AOL Instant Messenger became popular, I made my screen name some clever version of Jersey Girl. I was proud to be from the Garden State and not yet aware of what that sentiment actually meant. I yearned to return to my birthright and bided my time until I could.

All the same, Jersey was no more my home than Sacramento. Ironically, despite having two houses, I didn't consider any place to be "home." Much like my struggle to define my race, I struggled to find a place where I belonged. I was not only biracial; I was also bicoastal. With each trip,

I came to feel less like a child and more like a ping pong ball trapped in a long rally, longing for someone to miss me.

The summer after my freshman year in high school, my mom and stepdad separated. Eleven years of marriage down the drain, along with my whole "I'm immune to divorce" theory. Sad to say, when it comes to divorce, practice does not make perfect. Without guilt gifts, the second divorce proved much more difficult than the first. For with this development, I finally discovered the ugly side of divorce. Suddenly, I was forbidden to see my stepdad, who my mom now deemed dangerous.

"We don't know what he's capable of; I'm going to place a restraining order against him," she told me one night.

I couldn't fathom how she could be talking about my stepfather, the man who taught me how to ride a bike, built me a tree house, and kissed my boo-boos when I fell. Up until that point, he was the primary father figure in my life. I hardly knew or saw my real father. Her accusations didn't make sense, nor did I want them to. Believing her would mean that the man responsible for raising me was a monster. Not believing my mom would mean questioning her word on something grave, and believing that she too was a monster. Effectively, I decided that no one could be trusted. I declared myself an orphan and mentally quit them both.

In the end, the restraining order never held up in court, probably because there was too little to base it on. Still, it would be years before I could process what my mother told me and why. Back then I was too young to understand that realities are not ultimate truths but fluid concepts we can choose to create or accept. My mother has hers and I have mine. Once I had figured this out, my life appeared much more clearly, perhaps even more clearly than I wanted.

Finally, it all made sense why everything in my life had come in twos. My two birthdays, communions, everything; none of it was for me. It was all for her, my mom. Twenty-something years later, my mom still can't stand my dad and stepmom. Mention Julie's name, and like a reflex my mom will bark, "Who? The bitch who stole my husband?" To her, the words *Julie* and *bitch* are synonymous.

The more I thought about it, the more I realized perhaps I wasn't as unaffected by my parents' divorce as I once believed. Maybe my life was not like Noah's Ark, where having two of everything made sense. Come to think of it, my childhood wasn't exactly what you would call normal. In place of bedtime stories, I was told cautionary tales.

"Then one day Mommy got pregnant, but Daddy didn't want any more kids. But that didn't matter, because she had a miscarriage. The end!"

"What's a miscawage?"

"It's when a woman loses a baby, which is different from an abortion."

"What's an abwortion?" As a child I mixed up my w's and r's. Notwithstanding, I had an amazing vocabulary for a five-year-old.

Truly, I learned a lot from my mother. A huge proponent of honesty, my mom was always forthcoming about her relationships with both of my fathers. When she and my stepdad split up, she confided, "I only married Juan so that you would have a father." Instances like this are what helped me to recognize the difference between honesty and oversharing.

Nor did my mom ever miss an opportunity to remind me, or even strangers for that matter, of my father's "bad habits." Within five minutes of meeting one of my college boyfriends, a Muslim Resident Assistant, she managed to work in, "You know, Ali's father's side has a history of alcoholism." Frankly, it was the RA's fault. He had provoked her, commenting on how it was my twenty-first birthday and now I could legally drink.

As it was, I didn't have my first drink until I was well into college. In fact, it was practically legal. During high school I happily played the role of Sober Sally, lecturing my friends on why it was bad to drink or smoke, and driving them home when they did. I had no interest in drugs or alcohol, as my mom had effectively brainwashed me into thinking I was one sip away from having an addiction. "It runs in your family, you know."

This is her typical response when any of us have any ailment. When Monika and Kyle's baby fat didn't disappear, I suggested to my mom that we put them on a diet. "Well, you know Juan's side is big-boned," she responded, completely ignoring the fact that several members of her family are morbidly obese. When the "baby fat" turned into pre-diabetes, again she replied, "Well, I'm not surprised. It does run in Juan's family, you know." I shook my head thinking, your mother—my grandma—injected herself with insulin everyday because of Type 2 diabetes. You tasked *me* with taking grandma's blood sugar! I was eight! Looking back, it's not such bad parenting; the scare tactic worked for me. To this day, I'm petrified of addiction and certainly, diabetes.

According to my mom, our fathers were also responsible for our financial problems. I learned to never ask my mom for money. Instead I got a job cleaning houses. Nevertheless, the subject proved unavoidable.

"Can you drive me to Soraya's?"

"Ask her parents to pick you up."

"Why can't you drive me?"

"Because your dad (Juan) didn't pay me this month and I barely have enough money for groceries, let alone gas."

"Didn't you just get your nails done?"

"I'm a person too. God forbid I do anything for myself."

When money was tight and I needed to pay for college applications she told me to ask my father for help: "You have no idea how much money he owes me in back payments on your child support." I tried to picture my father the way she saw him, imagining this ATM machine drunkenly spitting out cash. The image alone still gives me the giggles.

After separating from my stepdad, my mom started dating again. However, this time I was old enough to protest. Watching your parents date is painful. I imagine this is why most people get married *before* having children, to spare their offspring from any unnecessary torture. While I expected to hate every man my mom brought home, I didn't expect her to make it so easy. Mostly, they were men she had met online: older white men with male-pattern baldness, spare-tire beer bellies, and one-syllable names that also doubled as foods— Chip, Stew, or Frank. As implied by their names, each one quickly expired.

Though I was the one in high school, my mom dated more often than I did. On Friday nights, my boyfriend Kenny and I would stay at home and watch TV, babysitting Monika and Kyle while my mom went out on dates, sometimes twice a night. She'd come home and say, "What-a-bore," then call up another suitor and make plans for another date, that same night. My mom's got game, what can I say?

In my mother's perpetual absence, I was at liberty to do as I pleased. Free of parental supervision, my house quickly became the designated party house. In retrospect, I have no idea why I didn't take more advantage of my situation and develop a drug habit or get pregnant, something a little more in keeping with what you read in the papers or see on TV. Regrettably, my friends and I were pretty boring. We were all honors students. Our shenanigans comprised of balloon fights, dinner parties, and the occasional movie night. The most badass we ever got was lying to my best friend's father, telling him, "Boys? No, we don't want any boys here," as our boyfriends cowered behind my couch.

Unlike most teens, vigilantly monitored by their parents and happy to be free of a watchful eye, I was terrified to be home alone. Nights when my mom was out and Monika and Kyle were with Juan, I'd sleep with a carving knife under my pillow, ready to shank any prowler. Our neighborhood was by no means dangerous, but after watching all those Lifetime movies about innocent girls getting killed by nighttime bedroom intruders, one begins to think. Okay, maybe I exaggerate when I say I slept with a knife under my pillow. For the truth is, I never slept.

My insomnia peaked in high school. I'd lie awake for hours, playing out all possible escape routes should anyone intrude. Every creak or tap at my window made me jerk. Must stay alert, I thought. Some nights, my fears would turn into panic attacks. When this happened, I often turned to prayer, reciting Hail Marys until I fell asleep. Eventually, I graduated high school, albeit sleep-deprived. Keeping my promise to myself, I returned to my beloved East Coast for college.

When I graduated from NYU, I made sure my parents attended two separate graduation ceremonies. It was exhausting, trying to figure out how to divvy up my time, but I did. It was well worth it too. Were my mother to encounter my stepmom, looking as young and beautiful as ever, my own personal World War III would have broken out. Now the only big event left to figure out will be my wedding, which in all probability won't happen for at least another decade or so, hopefully giving me just enough time to plan. By that time, I hope thirty years will accomplish what twenty years has not—acceptance. If not, I guess two weddings wouldn't be the worst thing in the world. More presents, right?

we might as well dance

Nobody likes being told they can't have something, even if it's something they don't actually want. It's like the feeling I get when somebody starts telling me a story, stops abruptly because they've said too much, and then shakes their head saying, "Oh, never mind."

"Come on, tell me. What? ... Why can't you tell me?"

Now the omission becomes a personal offense. Most people do it to provoke me, which is incredibly transparent and in my case, highly effective. I knowingly fall for it every time and yet I can't help myself. What? What did Sheryl say? As trivial as it may be, I need to know, regardless of whether I wanted to hear about it before. Really, it's a matter of principle. If you're going to start something then you sure as hell better finish it.

Alas, I'm not very convincing. Once I tried persuading a guy to fall in love with me, not because I loved him, but because I thought he should. It didn't work. Still I tried.

It all started when the guy I was dating told me, "I don't know if I love you." This was his response to an e-mail I sent him, expressing how much I cared about him, how I could see myself falling for him, and so forth. You get the drift. We had been dating a few months and I figured it was about time to say those three magic words. When another month came and went without them, I decided what he needed was a little encouragement. To my dismay, it was not encouragement he needed. "I'm just not passionate when it comes to people. My job, my country, sure I'm passionate, but people, not really. It's nothing personal. I'm like this with everyone," he told me. Perfect. Nothing personal. Just what every girl wants to hear.

While wedding bells weren't exactly ringing in my head, I felt wronged. He pursued me for a whole year, and for what? To finally win me over a year later and tell me I'm not sure I love you, but nothing personal? If anyone was justified in saying, "That's okay, I'll pass," it was me! When we first met I wanted nothing to do with him. He was a guy I met at a bar, during Fleet Week, and did I mention, a sailor? Nothing about the situation said true love. At best, he was an interesting anecdote for Sunday brunch.

Let me be clear, I was not out on the town scheming to pick up a sailor. I went to the bar to see my friend Stephanie, who was in town to see her brother, the Sailor. When I arrived Stephanie drunkenly threw her arms around me and dragged me to him, "This is Ali. She's a really good dancer. You should dance with her." Without words, he smiled, took me by the hand, and led me to the dance floor.

we might as well dance

At six-three, the Sailor was not built for grace. In fact, he was an aggressively bad dancer. Unlike most guys who can't dance and resign themselves to the two-step, he loved to dance and didn't let his inability prevent him from pulling out what he called "ALL the stops," which included twirling, dipping, and yes, getting low to the musical stylings of Lady Gaga, Ke$ha, and Katy Perry. Not surprisingly, he had a way of taking over the dance floor, as whenever we danced, he would swing me around like a wet rag. It was entertaining, to be sure. I laughed the whole time, knowing full well that we looked ridiculous, not caring that we did. Though he couldn't dance, the Sailor was debonair.

When I said goodbye he pulled me close as if to kiss me and asked me to stay. Tempted, I turned my cheek, hugged him, and gracefully bowed out. He was a sailor and it was Fleet Week. I've read Sign of the Chrysanthemum; I already know how that story ends.

After that, we saw each other three more times, whenever Stephanie was in town. Each time like the first, we'd dance, laugh, and at the end of the night he'd ask me to stay. I never did. Three words kept popping up in my head. "Stephanie's brother" and "sailor."

We'd talk now and then. He'd send me things from his travels—postcards and little trinkets. He was sweet and I can't deny I enjoyed, if not welcomed, the attention. In the end, his persistence won me over. A few months before I moved to Spain, we started dating, with Stephanie's enthusiastic blessing.

At first, he was so annoyingly perfect that I found myself searching for skeletons in his closet or weird fetishes. He was too normal, too well adjusted. I probed and snooped; however, the only thing I found even remotely abnormal was that he played Magic the Gathering, a nerdy card game to which I am no stranger. I too played Magic as a child, a detail I like to blame on my two older and more socially awkward brothers. Ultimately I had to face the fact that the Sailor was normal.

He wasn't my ideal guy but then again, my ideal guys weren't exactly working out, so I decided it was time to try something new. Unlike my ex, the Sailor was not goofy, tender, or playful. He was serious, levelheaded, and considerate, a complete departure from what I was used to, and I liked it. I was tired of catering to the emotional needs of artists and the sensitive types. Never again was a guy going to cry and ask me to hold him when I was upset and needed to be held. Besides, what's not to like about a tall, handsome, educated, well-traveled, and interesting man from a great and loving family? Hell, his father's a minister. Hands down, he was the type of guy you bring home to meet the folks.

I liked how easy things were with him. For one, we never fought. It's hard to get upset when someone is sitting in front of you, talking and acting completely rational. It started with little things. One time we were having sex and he finished before I did. Feeling that was unfair, I pitched a fit. Wise man that he is, he did not get his pride involved or inflate the issue. Instead he waited until I calmed down before casually addressing the issue, "About earlier, if you want me to go longer tell me and I will. But you have to tell me." We were in public—his friend's wedding—so I couldn't very well make a scene, not that I wanted to. I was too shocked by the frankness of his proposition.

"Oh, okay. Yeah." I said nodding my head, bewildered. What was I supposed to say? "No, I don't accept your reasonable solution! I won't tell you what I want next time!" His resolution shut me down before I had the opportunity to deny there was a problem so that I could bring it back up later.

Still, something felt off. The issue had been squashed and so I should have been jumping for joy, but instead I felt shortchanged. That's it? Fights were supposed to be difficult and draining, not easy and straightforward. Why didn't I feel more emotionally taxed? To be fair, the Sailor did most of the work. All I did was offer an "Okay." It was my first fight to ever get truly resolved.

From then on the precedent was set. Whenever I was bothered by something I did my best to tell him before it grew unmanageable. As always, he would remain calm, listen to what I had to say, and take time to reflect before responding. It was a perfect fit. He balanced me.

Yet as time went on, I began to read his levelheadedness differently, interpreting it as lack of emotion. We had no passion. I kept telling myself that it was a different type of relationship than I was used to, a slower one that simply needed patience and time. Still I couldn't ignore that we never laughed or had silly time, and even in our most intimate moments were never intimate. The Sailor and I didn't invent pet names for one another or share inside jokes. We didn't speak a secret language that only we could understand.

They say it's bad to compare relationships but I couldn't help myself. I missed Gums, my ex-boyfriend. Before we started dating, I used to tease him about his abnormally large smile that exposed more gums than teeth. In reality he had a great smile, but like a child I preferred to tease rather than compliment him. When we became a couple this eventually evolved into Gummy Bear and other saccharine derivatives that would make me queasy if coming from someone else's mouth. Though I tried to pretend that these things didn't matter, that I didn't want these things, I couldn't help but feel the Sailor and I were missing out on the best parts of a relationship.

Suddenly, I'd see other couples walking with their hands in each other's pockets on cold nights, all lovey dovey, and feel bitter. "Look at them, flaunting their love and happiness!" I'd seethe jealously. It was another reminder of what the Sailor and I didn't have. We had a good time together, but never a great time. Eventually, I concluded we made better business partners than lovers.

Nevertheless, his reply, "I'm not sure if I love you," caught me off guard. I expected to feel apathetic, or at the very most, irritated. Never did I expect I'd feel sad or worse, hurt. Sure, we may not have been in it for the long haul, yet saying it flat-out felt plain rude. I didn't necessarily see a future with him or even love him; but what did that matter? I wanted him to love me.

While I could easily list all the reasons why I didn't love him, I had no idea why he didn't love me. He was the first guy I dated who didn't instantly profess his undying love. Being a serial monogamist, I like to think I'm somewhat of a professional girlfriend. I cook, clean, cater to every whim, and love sex. Where had I gone wrong? The more I thought about it, the more convinced I was that he shouldn't just love me; damn it, he should want a future with me. I'm marriage material! Sure we were missing that certain je ne sais quoi, but that was on his end, not mine, right? Suddenly, I found myself wanting more and wanting him to want more. It wasn't rational, but when has that ever stopped me?

Unfortunately, trying to convince the Sailor to fall in love with me didn't go as I imagined. In the end, the only person who fell in love was, well, me. If anything, my efforts only managed to worsen my situation from insignificant to pathetic. What was once a relationship in which no one was in love quickly turned into a sad case of unrequited love. I quickly discovered that love is like a pair of shoes; it only works if you have two. One is just silly. So there I was, a stinky lonely shoe who thought she was in love because she wanted someone who she didn't love to love her. Karma perhaps.

Rational Ali would admit it wasn't his fault. He was only being honest and if I had been honest I would've said, "I don't know if I want a future with you either." Knowing me, however, it would have sounded more like, "Just because I don't want a relationship with you, doesn't give you the right to not want a relationship with me. So what if I don't love you? You still need to love me!" Looking back, I'm glad I didn't say anything because sometimes when you say how you really feel in a moment of passion, it sounds ridiculous. More importantly, it probably wouldn't have gone over well. I wasn't ready to be honest with him or me. I wanted it both ways. The more I thought about it, the more desperate I became for him to love me, but demanding that someone love you isn't attractive and probably why it doesn't usually work.

Incidentally, this was not the first time someone told me there was no possibility of a future. You'd think I would learn from the past, but that's giving me way too much credit. If I excel at anything, it's at repeating my mistakes. I reacted as badly the second time as I did the first time, and if there's a third time—because who am I kidding?—I'm sure I'll react just the same. In the spring of my junior year of college I dated the Muslim RA who, after our first kiss, said, "We can't get married." My head cocked back instinctually, giving him a confused stare as if to suggest, did I miss something?

"...because you're not Muslim," he clarified.

Dumbfounded, I remained silent. What was I supposed to say? We were twenty, making marriage the last thing on my mind. If anything, I had been thinking, I like kissing. I want to kiss some more. Not, I love you, let's get married! Still in a state of confusion, I stammered, "Okay." Why the red flags didn't go up then … well, let's just say I was preoccupied. He was a good kisser!

Naturally, the relationship progressed, and predictably we fell in love. For the next few months I did everything I could to show that I supported his culture. My entire summer was spent learning about Bangladesh and reading Islam for Dummies at Barnes & Noble. Every meal was Halal. I even participated in Ramadan and agreed to go a month without my two favorite things, food and sex. Talk about sacrifice. In spite of my efforts, the finality of those words, "We can't get married," constantly loomed over us, reminding us that it was only a matter of time.

You'd be surprised how often the topic came up. Once we were lying in bed after having sex and I asked him, "What are you thinking?" The point of the question wasn't to provoke some life-altering conversation, but rather to fill the awkward silence that can sometimes follow sex. His response, "Oh, you know, how I'll have to answer for this on Judgment Day." This should have been my cue for the door, a clothes on in record time, never call me again, nice knowing you kind of exit. Judgment Day is not my idea of pillow talk. However, I stayed.

The next day I met a friend for coffee. "He said WHAT?" she shrieked, her mouth hanging agape. I repeated it once more and laughed. Judgment Day. After all, this hadn't really happened. It was just some crazy dream. How could I not laugh? I waited for her to yell at me, talk some sense into me, but she didn't. I'd have to do it on my own. How did I get myself into this situation? All I wanted was a kiss and now I'm in a dead-end relationship with a guy who considers me a sin. Brilliant.

"You don't appreciate everything I do for you," he complained from the other side of my door, which I refused to open for him. It was our fifth fight that week and I needed some space.

"I don't need you to do nice things for me. You could give me a piece of paper cut up into a snowflake and I'd be happy," I tried to assure him. The next day I woke up to twenty paper snowflakes slid under my door. Not at all what I meant, I thought as I shook my head. But how could I expect him to understand me? We spoke two different languages: he the Koran, and I the Satanic Verses.

A few days later, he and I gathered enough sense between the two of us to break up, which was followed by a succession of failed "let's get back together" attempts. Once a masochist, always a masochist. We were broken from the start and stood no chance of being mended. After a while we had no choice but to accept defeat. We finally broke up for good. It would be two years before he would speak to me again.

Were I more mature, I would have agreed with the Sailor. "I don't really see a future for us either, but let's enjoy the time we have together, shall we?" I'd smile; we'd hold hands and go off to enjoy the rest of our afternoon, not in love. It's not that I don't understand that relationships sometimes don't work out. It's just, if that's the case, then I'd prefer it to be my idea. I don't deal well with boundaries, so the minute I find one, I bail.

Sad thing is, I know better. I can hear the sound of my grandfather's voice over and over in my head, "Well, it may not be the party you had hoped for, but since we're here, we might as well dance." It's an expression he uses often when he wants to remind me to enjoy what I've been given, even if it isn't quite what I expected or wanted. However, acceptance is easier said than done. I try to enjoy things for what they are, but pretending to be fine with something you're not actually fine with is just as impossible as pretending to love someone, or worse, forcing someone to love you. It doesn't feel quite right, and everyone knows you're faking.

I'm sure if I told the Sailor it was over, he'd be hurt and ask for an explanation. "Because you've made it entirely clear that we have no future and you don't love me," I'd say. I of course never said any of these things because in truth, he neither promised me nor denied me love. Rather, he offered me here and now. Just as he couldn't be sure he loved me, I couldn't be sure I didn't love him. Maybe it wasn't love, maybe it was never going to be love, but it was closer to love than anything else. I found someone who cared about me enough to be honest, brutally honest. It hurt and it certainly wasn't what I wanted to hear. My pride was bruised. Ultimately I decided, whether he loved me or not, I was going to stay. Because if I had learned anything from my previous relationship, it's that we fall, even when we don't intend to.

a beautiful mess

At an early age, I learned how to make the most of my education. In kindergarten, I convinced my friend Brandy to help me trap a boy under a table because I wanted to kiss him. Billy was my first crush. He had blond hair, dimples, and like myself, was a Mickey Mouse fan. The plan was simple—isolate and attack. I told him I found a cool toy under the table and without hesitation, he gladly followed me under. Once below, I signaled Brandy to push in all the chairs, thereby trapping us underneath. Before he could notice there was no toy, I grabbed Billy by the face and planted my first kiss. I smiled, taking in the sweet taste of victory, which as it turns out is apple juice. I wish I could say that over the years my methods of luring men have become more sophisticated. Unfortunately, they've worsened.

I pity the fools who try to go out with me. Dating me is like converting to Judaism. On average, I reject a guy three times before deciding I might like him. If he's still interested after the third attempt, I figure he's at least earned a date. I wish I could say I'm playing hard to get; however, that would imply that I have a strategy and know what I'm doing. Nothing could be further from the truth. At twenty-five, I am still as much of a novice as I was at five.

My mixed signals probably don't help, either. Understandably, telling someone you "just want to be friends" usually is girl code for "try harder." Plus, when girls say "it's fine," it's not actually fine, and when we say, "no," sometimes that means "yes" (except when it's rape). Perhaps this is why Gums refused to take "no" for an answer, knowing that by "no," what I actually meant was "not now."

A few months before we started dating, I showed up at his door, soaking wet from the rain. It sounds cliché because it was. As a senior in college, most of my understanding of relationships came from watching romantic comedies. Unable to stay away, I told myself that I had to see him. We needed to discuss the future of our relationship—a ridiculous concept, considering we weren't dating. But we were children then, pretending to be adults by doing what we thought was right— talking. It would be years before both of us would realize, talking doesn't accomplish much of anything unless you really know what you want and are ready to be honest about it. In this case, he was ready. I wasn't. So we sat for hours on his couch, a brown secondhand pullout that also doubled as his bed in his living room, talking in circles.

"It'll never work... you're too much like my ex," I told him, referring to Sean, a high school sweetheart from Sacramento.

"I'm not your ex, Ali."

"Yeah, and I'd like to keep it that way. If we date, we'll break up and then our friendship will be ruined."

"I don't want to be your friend. I'm never going to just be your friend. I'm always going to want more. We belong together."

"You only think I'm great because you haven't dated me. I'm stubborn, needy, and I throw tantrums. Plus, I always need to get my way."

"I have sisters. Trust me, I know how to handle women. Plus, you'll always get your way with me."

Immediately what came to mind was, this guy is crazy! Another one for the list—Reasons Why You Cannot Date Gums, No. 15: Welcomes dysfunctional people in his life, i.e. me. No matter what I said, he just sat there calmly, with a smug smile on his face, ready to refute my every rebuttal. Jerk. His persistence was flattering and yet contemptible, his tenacity I first loved and then came to hate. I couldn't tell whether I wanted to kiss him or yell at him for not listening to me.

Though I wasn't ready to admit it, Gums was everything I wanted in a guy. He met every neurotic requirement: oldest child from a big family, good with children, funny, same taste in clothes, books, music, and food. On paper, it was a match made in heaven. But that was the problem. He was too perfect, and therefore untrustworthy.

Exasperated by the conversation, I told him, "It's just not a good idea," and left. Clearly, I was getting nowhere and Gums was a glutton for punishment. However, like it or not, he was right. I just had a lover's spat with a guy I supposedly didn't want to date. It was too late to be friends. I was invested. I didn't know then and wouldn't until two months later, he had already won. He had wormed his way into my life and my heart. I never stood a chance.

I'm not going to say it was love at first sight. However, from the moment we saw each other, there was a palpable chemistry. Something drew me to him and at the risk of sounding like a Danielle Steel novel, I found myself in the meet-cute of a chick flick. Time slowed. The crowd blurred. In my head, the song Overjoyed by Stevie Wonder started playing in the background. Suddenly, I felt desperate to know who he was. Corny, I know, but that's how it happened.

To be fair, any girl would have felt the same way. Even back then people crowded themselves around him because it was obvious he was going to be "somebody." He was gorgeous, but not in the conventional way, so he didn't see what other people saw, making him humble and personable. More than attractive, Gums was talented. As a performer, he knew very well how to be funny and entertain a crowd. Thus, he was the type of person you quoted at parties, because more than anything Gums was charming, and it was this charm that drew people to emulate him.

Not that any of those things truly mattered to me. Actually, what lured me to him was the way he looked at me. The first time we saw each other he smiled warmly, as if I were a friend he hadn't seen in a while, a look that said, "Hey, it's good to see you. I've missed you." It was so natural and sincere that without intending to, I smiled back, "Likewise." He and I had never met, and yet he felt strangely familiar.

It was the August before my junior year of college and like most RAs, I was participating in a weeklong preparation course. I spotted Gums on the second day into training. Both too shy to talk to one another, we exchanged a series of sweet yet awkward glances in the cafeteria. Verbal contact didn't occur until a week after training, at a party called the Beach Ball, which all freshmen RAs were obligated to attend.

Like Billy, my kindergarten kiss, I had a plan for Gums. Another RA in my building, Ronnie, was a good friend of Gums. All I had to do was hang out with Ronnie and wait for Gums to come to me.

Halfway through my stakeout, there was no sign of Gums. Ready to give up, I excused myself to use the bathroom and when I came out, there he was, standing next to Ronnie. While I was happy to see him, his timing couldn't have been worse. Having never formally met, Gums introduced himself and offered to shake my hand. Normally, this would have been fine. However, as it was, I had just come from the bathroom and my hands were still cold and damp from washing. Nobody likes shaking a wet hand, least of all me with my crush. I don't care if the hand belongs to the Queen of England or the Dalai Lama; it feels gross. Knowing they're clean doesn't offer much comfort either. The only thing I can think of is, one of us just peed. In this case, I was the pee-er. Stupid bladder, I lamented.

Not wanting to make a scene, I shook his hand while muttering an apology. Confused, he pursed his lips and squinted at me. What for? Hoping to clarify, I said, "My hands are still wet from the bathroom... don't worry, I washed them." I should have stopped there, but instead I kept going, "Usually, I avoid wearing a one-piece bathing suit, because they're such a hassle to pee in." Awesome start, Ali. Earlier that night as I got dressed, I had imagined us talking about many things; my urine was not one of them.

To my surprise, he laughed and asked, "Did you pull it to the side like little girls do at the beach?" Cupping his hand, he reached down, and mimicked pulling the crotch of an imaginary bathing suit to the side while hopping around like a kid on hot sand. His candor caught me off guard, as did his familiarity with how to pee in a woman's one-piece. I laughed and immediately knew I was in trouble. This one wouldn't scare easy.

a beautiful mess

Ours was a slow start. This was mostly my fault, or technically, my boyfriend's fault for standing in our way. At the time, I had just rekindled my romance with Sacramento Sean. Rather than recognize my chemistry with Gums as a sign that I didn't love Sean, I decided to stay in my comfortable relationship for another eight months. Meanwhile, Gums and I would have weekly run-ins around campus and make small talk about cafeteria food as a way of ignoring our attraction. Luckily, Sean and I broke up later that spring. Shortly thereafter, Gums and I had our first date.

I invited him over to play Mario Kart and when we got hungry, I suggested we go to my favorite Thai restaurant in SoHo. When the check came, he paid the twenty-dollar tab with his babysitting money. Then like a gentleman, he "walked me home," or as we like to say in NYC, rode the subway with me, passed his stop, and dropped me off in front of my apartment.

Anyone who has watched a movie or read a book knows what came next. Smiling, Gums leaned in and kissed me tenderly, as in, without tongue. I remember thinking that it lacked luster. After months and months of dancing around this attraction I half-expected it to feel something more along the lines of an I Can't Believe It's Not Butter commercial, the definition of true romance. Instead, it was more... eh. Not bad, but needs improvement. To be fair, my mind was elsewhere.

Three weeks prior to my date with Gums I started seeing the Muslim RA in my building. That's right, Mr. Judgment Day himself. People say timing is everything and in this case it was. That winter was one of the hardest times in my life. I was going through a lot of family problems when one night while out with friends, the RA kissed me and I kissed him back. Whether it was the alcohol or my pent up emotions, I'm not sure. All I knew was that it made me feel something I hadn't felt in a long time: happy. The rest just snowballed from there.

Anyhow, in an effort to make things between us "casual," the Muslim RA suggested I see other people. Taking his advice, I went on a date with Gums. Poor clueless Gums didn't know any of this when he kissed me. Nor had I any reason to tell him; we had only gone on one date, a good one at that.

The Muslim RA just happened to be crossing the street when he came upon Gums and I in our liplock. Proving just how un-casual things actually were between us, the RA angrily ran inside the dorm, but not before shooting me a look of pained fury. "So, I'll call you!" I awkwardly and quickly told Gums as I ran after the Muslim RA.

Once inside the building, the RA confronted me. "He doesn't really care about you, Ali. You're just another notch on his belt!" he screamed, tears streaming down his face. He cried. I cried. Then we started dating. Healthy.

The next day, Gums called to apologize for the unexpected kiss, and asked if I wanted to be exclusive. He sounded so sweet, so innocent, so... so... desperate. His jump from our first kiss to a monogamous relationship scared the shit out of me. Plus, it wasn't a good time, since now there was the RA to consider. Not wanting to complicate things, I told Gums flat-out, "There's someone else." Crushed, he didn't speak to me for most of the summer. He graduated and I started my last year in college.

That winter, after things with the RA officially ended, Gums called and asked me to hang out. I hadn't seen or heard much from him after that summer. He graduated and started working. As for me, I tried to keep my distance out of respect for the RA, who still hadn't forgotten about the little kiss. Still, we'd talk now and then; as hard as we tried to cut ties, even back then, Gums and I couldn't go more than two months without contacting one another.

Though I wanted to see him, the idea made me pause, knowing that this was no simple invitation to hang out. Unable to resist temptation, I told him, "Sure."

Still pretending to be uninterested, I didn't bother changing out of my sweats or looking in a mirror. I have unfortunately high self-esteem, allowing me to delude myself into thinking I look good all the time, even in sweats. Not to mention that the last thing I wanted to do was give him the impression I was trying; that would be leading him on. I quickly learned the error of my ways. Regardless of who is coming over, you should always take a second to look in a mirror.

The first thing he said was, "What's wrong with your face?"

"That's mean."

"No really, what's wrong with it?" he asked as he reached over and plucked a small piece of toilet paper from my forehead, a mini-Japanese flag. Earlier I used a piece of toilet paper to stop a popped pimple from bleeding and had forgotten about it. Humiliated, I buried my face in my hands and doubled over into the fetus position. I wanted to hide, shrink, or if possible, turn invisible. Trying to regain composure, I stood up but all I could do was laugh, awkwardly.

When embarrassed or uncomfortable, my immediate reaction is to laugh uncontrollably, with serious full belly laughs that force you to grab your stomach and go red in the face. In a crowded place like New York City, my quirk is easily camouflaged, as my surroundings typically offer more entertainment than a girl laughing to herself. However, when alone in a room, face to face with the guy you're sort of maybe interested in, it can be both problematic and unfortunate.

Had I any control over my laughter, I would have played it cool, pretended to be the type of girl who can laugh at herself or doesn't take life too seriously. Alas, I'm not that girl. I'm a girl who laughs when she's embarrassed, so my laughter continued well past the point of being fun or socially acceptable. Leave it to me to take an already uncomfortable moment and make it even more painfully awkward. It was a vicious cycle. The longer I laughed, the more awkward it became, and so finally

I managed to choke back my laughs as I coughed from a dry throat. As we walked to my couch, wide-eyed, I mouthed to the air, "FUCK!" Strangely, he thought nothing of it. He found the toilet paper and my laughter endearing.

Some weeks later, we kissed for the second time. It was almost a year since our first kiss; this time, I was completely single. To this day I maintain that he tricked me. He called me late one night after getting off work and asked, "What are you doing? I've had a bad day. Can we get a drink?" He sounded really upset, angry even. When he came over I handed him a glass of wine; he grabbed the bottle and proceeded to chug. His behavior was completely out of character, and it intrigued me. Slamming the empty bottle on my counter, he barked, "Let's go to a bar." One drink later, we were both drunk and putting on airs.

"I'm so over you," he slurred. "I'm finally over you."

"Like hell you are." I slurred back.

Sure enough, by the end of the night we were curled up on a couch, kissing. Who's over who now, I thought, followed by, oh wait. Suddenly, I realized this had been his plan all along. Well played, sir. Well played.

As the courting continued, so did my mortification. Two weeks later I took Gums to my favorite bakery in the East Village. Having almost identical palates, he ordered my personal favorite, a lemon tart topped with fresh berries. On principle, I avoid ordering the same thing as my dining partner since I make it a habit to eat from both our plates. This way I get to order what I want, as well as the thing I want second most. Not that there was any doubt in my mind. There was a certain dessert I had been eyeing for weeks, a chocolate mousse served in a giant chocolate teacup, topped with cream, berries, and a chocolate music note. So beautiful, so decadent, it was hardly a dessert to eat alone. I relished the opportunity to finally try it.

After sitting down, I daintily picked up the teacup by its chocolate handle, extending my pinky (naturally), and took a bite. Had I taken a second to think, I might have realized the following: real teacups are usually used for sipping, not biting, and chocolate teacups in general are more fragile than regular teacups. To no one's surprise but my own, the cup broke, catapulting the mousse onto my face.

Everything from the bridge of my nose down to my chin was covered in a thick layer of chocolate mousse. Instinctually, my hands shot up as I attempted to shield myself. Like him or not, I had no intention of letting him see me in chocolate-face. Thankfully, when it happened, Gums was still looking down at his tart. He glanced up, only to see me cowering behind my hands as I screamed, "Napkin!"

How do I manage such feats? I sulked, waiting for him to grab some napkins. True to form, Gums remained calm. With a handful of napkins, he lowered my hands, and gently wiped my face clean. "You're a mess," he said, "but a beautiful one."

He was the first guy to see me for who I am, and call me by name. I knew in that moment that I'd love him forever.

When it comes to relationships, there is an unspoken agreement between men and women that obligates a man to tell a woman she's beautiful, regardless of how she looks. If they're smart, they'll know that the truth isn't worth the hassle of, "What did you mean by that?" As Gums' first girlfriend I expected to do my fair share of training. However, I happily discovered that Gums never hesitated or needed prompting to tell me I was beautiful. In fact, "perfect" was the word he'd use, and always with a sincere tone. "You're my dream girl," he said, as we lay in the grass of Union Square Park. Cynic that I am, I quipped back, "Only until you have another dream."

A year after we broke up, I asked Gums if he remembered any of these embarrassing incidents. He didn't. Why would he? He was never the one affected by my insecurities or quirks. I was the one who made it a point to feel uncomfortable. After reminding him of all the mortifying moments, he said, "Oh. Yeah. Those things don't matter when you really love someone. I wanted to understand you, and so I did."

"You didn't know that you loved me then."

"Yes I did. Everything I wrote, thought about, was you. I've always loved you."

It was that simple. Turns out I didn't need to warn him about my many flaws in advance. He knew who I was long before I did. Somehow, Gums always loved me in spite of being a beautiful mess.

the mac 'n' cheese war

A friend's mother once told me that in India, people ask what you ate for lunch as a way of making small talk. There, food is considered a benign topic. Clearly, she's never met my father. A man who would sooner disgrace his dead mother than renounce his love of food.

It was Christmas Day and as usual my family was gathered at my father's for the annual Christmas brunch. I was standing in the living room talking to my cousins when, from the kitchen, I heard my father shouting (this is his normal voice), "I'm telling you, Mom didn't know what she was doing. That's not how you make mac 'n' cheese. Well, real mac 'n' cheese."

"What are you talking about? She used milk, pasta, and cheese. How's that not mac 'n' cheese?" my aunt cried.

"It's not her fault. She used the recipe from the original The Joy of Cooking, which was wrong. Real mac 'n' cheese calls for a béchamel. Mom didn't use a béchamel. She didn't know."

"So you're telling me, what we ate growing up wasn't real mac 'n' cheese? That our dead mother didn't know how ta make REAL mac 'n' cheese?"

There are certain things you should never say to a person. One of them is "Your mom can't cook." Dead or alive, regardless of the kind of relationship you have with your mother, it's considered poor taste. I'm not sure for how many months my aunt and uncle stopped talking to my father, but when we did eventually see them again, the subject was hardly old news.

Tact is not my father's strong suit. When I was sixteen he told me, "Ali, you're beautiful, but you'd be much prettier if you didn't have such bad acne." His intention wasn't to make me feel bad. To the contrary, his concern was the effect my skin would have on my self-esteem. Parents caution their children all the time. Don't sit too close to the TV. Don't eat too many sweets. Or in my case, maybe see a doctor about your complexion. This may seem harsh to some, but now that I'm older I'm glad my father didn't coddle me. I encounter tactless people all the time and rather than take offense, I take comfort in their words, knowing it's coming from a place of love, or at the very least, concern.

Not surprisingly, desecrating my late grandmother's mac 'n' cheese was not the first offensive thing my father said that day. Earlier my Uncle Rich and Aunt Beth arrived with a dish, which upon examining, my dad exclaimed, "What's wrong with the kielbasa?"

"Oh, I saw a recipe online and thought it looked interesting."

"You don't put cranberries in kielbasa! What were you thinking? Good thing I made my own."

Normally, when someone brings a dish for dinner it's considered a kind gesture. However, in my dad's mind, my aunt crossed a line, one separating ordinary food and that which is sacred. Take my sushi, take my taco, but don't mess with my kielbasa. That which is sacred to my father includes any and every family dish, or at least a dish he's mastered. It is a line he vehemently guards. Once he tried to argue with my stepmom and I about the correct way to make lumpia, a Filipino egg roll—mind you, he's Polish and German. His expertise knows no bounds.

Each night, after all the dishes have been put away, my father will pour himself a glass of Chardonnay, sit in his leather recliner, and chastise cooking shows: "What are you doing? That's not how you do it!" It's crossed my mind to tell him, "You know, Emeril can't really hear you, right?" But that would take away all my fun.

I suppose it comes with the territory. After working for more than twenty years in the food industry my father has morphed into something of a food idiot savant. He knows everything there is to know about food, restaurants, and those involved. If he had Asperger's, his quirk would be naming the precise location of every product in our local ShopRite. If you really wanted to mess with him, you'd ask the store manager to rearrange all the aisles.

On Fridays, my father will write his grocery list, two pages of illegible words scribbled on a yellow legal pad, in the exact order of the store's layout, aisle by aisle. Produce first, milk last. As he writes, his face is almost identical to that of a child writing to Santa Claus, and I'm forced to believe that he puts an extraordinary amount of thought into his list. One would think this methodology expedites grocery shopping; yet, I've never seen the man spend less than two hours at a supermarket. Irrespective of the items on his list, he likes to walk down every aisle and see what's been added, replaced, or is out of stock.

He buys more food than two people could ever consume, as it is just he and my stepmother now. Though, looking in his pantry, you'd wonder why he bothers going shopping at all. His pantry is always fully stocked. In college I'd come home once a month and go grocery shopping—in his cupboards. Just about any farm animal you can imagine is stored in his fridge. Once my brothers and I discussed signing him up for the A&E show Intervention. Alas, to take away my father's grocery shopping would be to take away his livelihood. My father looks forward to his weekly grocery shopping like a child eagerly awaits Saturday morning cartoons.

Besides, his grocery shopping pales in comparison to his cooking habits, which also must be executed in a precise manner. With all of us having masters' degrees, you'd think my brothers and I would know how to cut a cucumber. Turns out, we don't. Cucumbers must first be cut in half (lengthwise), with its seeds removed. And only then, cut into half moons, because everyone knows the seeds make the salad mushy. As his sous chefs, my brothers and I will hold up the first slice of every vegetable to my father, awaiting his approval before proceeding. It sounds excessive and it is, but what other alternative do we have? If we didn't help my father cook we'd end up eating the world's most extravagant salad for dinner at two a.m. Each meal takes at least three hours to prepare, no matter how simple or complex it may be. Asking him to change his ways now is like asking a dog to pee without lifting its leg. You're just fighting nature.

Watching him cook, I'm convinced he hates the environment since he insists on covering every surface in our entire kitchen with paper towels and foil. "Makes cleanup easier," he'll say. Yes, this too is another area of expertise—cleanup. Don't even think about putting something away in Tupperware; he'll just transfer it to another, then make you wash the one you dirtied. He has an uncanny knack for finding the best-fitting Tupperware. Every time!

I always warn my boyfriends about my father's quirks the first time I take them home. Generally, when most girls say,

"Listen, there's a few things you should know about my dad," the statement is followed by something like, "He's a Giants fan so don't mention the Jets," or "He's really into hunting so don't mind the taxidermy."

Never are my boyfriends expecting me to say, "He talks to himself ... well, more like curses to himself in the mirror after he showers, and sometimes while he's cooking alone in the kitchen. Oh, and late at night, he goes to the bathroom in the dark with the door open, so if you walk in on him peeing, don't worry, happens all the time. Most importantly, he's very particular about how he cooks so forget whatever you think you know about cutting vegetables and just go with it."

Then I'll add, "But he was in 'Nam, so..." as if this explains everything. Usually, they'll stay quiet and I'll accept their non-response as their consent. In reality, I know their silence is simply a way to fill time, wondering if it's too late to back out. Typically, it is. They figure the bit about vegetables is a joke and when they arrive, are surprised to learn it's not. Amused by my father's dedication to food, they're patient as my father instructs them on how to properly cut an onion, while he educates them on the difference between a roux and béchamel.

Though a writer, my father isn't much of a storyteller. Mention a duck, however, and he'll tell you about the time his grandmother Sophie gave him and his brothers a couple of baby ducks to raise.

"'So there we were, at my Grandma's house for Easter and we say, 'Grandma, where's our ducks you gave us at Christmas?' and she goes, 'They flew away!' So my mother leans over and says, 'You wanna know where your duck is? Look at your plate!'" Afterwards, he'll grab his chest and laugh so hard that his face will turn the same shade of red as his suspenders. This is one of the three stories my father tells.

He'll offer up other morsels of information here and there, like how his grandfather would eat butter and pepper sandwiches because he was so poor, suggesting that this long-lost relative and I are clearly related since for whatever reason, we've chosen the same snack. "Now isn't that something," my dad remarked as I bit into my poor man's sandwich. "Yaw, r-eal intre-shing," I replied, mouth full.

Most of his stories involve food and simpler times. Everything else is off the table, especially topics my father deems "too morose," like Diane, his first wife and late mother to Michael and Brian. Outside of cooking, gardening, and sports, I don't know much about what my father thinks.

Generally, my father is quiet and methodical, with a stern countenance that never lets you know exactly what he's thinking. Put him in front of a leg of lamb, however, and he's a kid who just heard the ice cream truck. Surrounded by fruits, vegetables, and spices, he's animated and some might even say talkative. Although every conversation revolves around food, if I'm patient, he'll throw in a personal anecdote and I get a glimpse into the man I crave to know better. Consequently, I've learned that if I wanted to communicate with him, I needed to learn food.

Despite his anal retentive ways, and moans and groans, my father enjoys having my brothers and I help him in the kitchen. In fact, growing up, he would demand our help while he cooked. At the time, I saw it as a form of indentured servitude. I was too young to understand that it was really just an excuse for him to keep us close. By inviting us to cook, he was inviting us into his world, knowing that what is shared in a meal is much more than food. Conceivably, this is why I consider cooking synonymous with acts of love. It's a mundane act but a form of intimacy nonetheless.

Now that we're older, Christmas is the only time when my brothers and I are all home. Hence, it's my father's favorite holiday, as this gives him an excuse to cook and entertain. In all the excitement, he'll take off work the day before to do all the shopping and cooking, making sure, of course, to buy almost everything in the store. This wouldn't be a problem except that he'll buy more food than our two refrigerators can hold. Consequently, the garage acts as our third fridge during the holidays. Truth be told, my brothers and I can eat our fair share of food, a talent we inherited from our father, who can down a whole ear of corn in one breath. Like a typewriter, he'll chomp row by row, kernels flying in the air, as his face turns red from lack of oxygen. He won't stop until the cob is white and bare. My boyfriends often wonder why I eat like a savage. Then they meet my father.

From the time we get up in the morning to the time we go to sleep, my family is in the kitchen eating. We even eat while we cook. My brothers will cut perfect cucumbers for our salad while I slice salami and cheese for an in-between-meal snack. Essentially, it's a marathon of eating and drinking. Come to think of it, I've never seen my kitchen table without food. To my father, our homecoming is not a simple get-together, it's a mission to make sure no one leaves hungry and without at least three Tupperware containers of leftovers. Every year he'll complain that we swipe his Tupperware but he loves it because it gives him a reason to buy some more at ShopRite.

Before we arrive, my father will send out an e-mail, which never fails to sound formal. Casual is something my father doesn't do. I can't help but feel like I'm reading an e-mail from an employer. Please let me know what your itinerary is for this weekend. Even his parting comment, love Dad, feels impersonal.

In the e-mail, he'll instruct us on the time and the official menu, even though neither changes year to year. As if baiting us, he'll invite us to bring a dish; however, I know this is just a polite gesture. Offer to bring dessert and he'll still make his own. The same, even. He'll turn it into a competition, as if it were an episode of Bobby Flay's Throwdown. Michael once told my dad he wanted to bring pecan pie, and after interrogating my brother on how he intended to make the pie, my dad decided he too would prepare his own. Rather than tell my brother he didn't approve of his recipe, my father turned dessert into a pie contest.

My stepmom and I were forced to judge and after sampling both pies, we agreed on a diplomatic tie. When we announced the results, my father nodded his head approvingly. Win or lose, it didn't matter to my father. Mac 'n' cheese or pecan pie; at the end of the day my father's priority is not the food, but rather the company it brings.

the sweetest goodbye

After Diane passed away, her parents, Rita and Guy, made it a point to actively participate in raising their grandchildren, my two older brothers Michael and Brian. When their father remarried and had me, Rita and Guy took me in too. Now a part of Michael and Brian's lives, I guess they figured I was a part of theirs as well. That's how Rita became my grandma.

As a child, I was too young to understand my relationship to Rita. Consequently, I spent the better half of my childhood thinking I was Italian. While I am many things, Italian is not one of them. Honorary Italian, maybe. Although it may sound like an oxymoron, I had a rather wholesome Jersey-Italian upbringing. Rather than sleep with the fishes, we ate them—seven to be exact—for the Feast of the Seven Fishes, an Italian custom celebrated on Christmas Eve. This was often coupled with listening to my favorite Christmas song, Dominick the Christmas Donkey. On Sunday afternoons, we played Bocce in the yard. Every Easter, Grandma would make her famous handmade manicotti.

Like any Italian grandma, or any grandmother, really, Rita could always be found in the kitchen, whipping up something delectable. In fact, her food was so delicious that anything she made ceased to be known by its general name. Eggplant parmesan was rechristened Rita's eggplant parm, because to call it anything less would be sacrilegious. No one cooked like Grandma. As the chef of our house, I'm sure my dad loved hearing all of us yell, "Make it like Grandma!"

Judging by the way she cooked, you'd think she'd be heavier. However, Rita was short and petite and dressed in a way that was both flattering and modest. She was always well put together, the kind of woman who wears pearls, heels, and a full face of makeup just to weed the garden. While I struggle to brush my teeth every morning, my grandma's grace was effortless.

Eventually, I figured out that Rita and I were not blood-related. Rita was not my dad's mom or my mom's mom. Still, as a child, I never questioned our relationship. Rita was my grandmother. Like any other grandchild, she showered me with kindness and gifts.

One Christmas she gave me this stuffed-animal cat. It looked so real that for years I would tell people we had a cat named Tabitha, who I kept in a box under my bed. Grandma had wrapped the box Tabitha came in so beautifully that I kept it. This became Tabitha's home, which Grandma helped me to decorate, sewing Tabitha a mini-pillow and bedspread. While

I know my grandma loved me, I'm sure she was this kind and considerate to everyone. That's just my Grandma, a true lady in every way.

Growing up I didn't see much of my grandma. Or, perhaps it's better to say that I didn't see her as much as I would have liked. My parents divorced when I was a year old, so at best, I saw my father every other weekend. This was when my mom's family and I still lived in Jersey. Once we moved to California, my already infrequent visits deteriorated to only twice a year. Still, no matter where I lived, Grandma always sent me a card for my birthday and every national holiday, along with five dollars. Whenever I came to my father's house, the only home I've managed to keep my entire life, she'd always set aside time just for me.

One summer when I was sixteen, I remember she took me out for a grandmother-granddaughter date. Sparing no expense, Grandma treated me to all the fine perks that Jersey has to offer—eating out, the movies, and shopping. For lunch we went to this quaint little Italian place in the old part of town. I ordered the eggplant sandwich thinking it would be like Grandma's, but it wasn't. It was cold and its texture resembled plastic, but not wanting to offend my grandma, I ate it. Afterwards we watched America's Sweethearts, as per my suggestion. She wanted to see Legally Blonde, yet I protested, telling her it looked like a flop. Incorrect. Before dropping me off, we went shopping at some department store. There I picked up a Winnie the Pooh poem about sisters. Grandma convinced me to buy it, saying it would be a nice thing to do for my sister. She was right. I felt so happy as we left the store, imagining Monika's face upon presenting it to her. That was it, just a simple day shared between a grandma and her granddaughter.

Six hours later, our home phone rang. I didn't need to hear the conversation. My dad's face said it all. It was a face I had seen before, first when it was Uncle Tommy, and then Uncle Robert. The latter call had come on my dad's birthday. Poor dad. Imagine having your own brother die on your birthday.

"What happened?" I asked, dreading yet half expecting to hear my Uncle Rich's name.

"Grandma's in the hospital. She had a stroke."

Five hours later, she passed away. I should have cried, but I didn't. It hurt, but then again it didn't. Really, I consider myself fortunate. I didn't have to watch her disintegrate in a hospital bed, or experience the pain of her slowly forgetting who I am. I didn't have to worry about what were the last words I said to her. They were "I love you," said as I kissed her cheek and hopped out of the car. My last memory of my grandma involves nothing but happiness, time spent free of the looming dread that comes with knowing what little time you have left. I didn't know it was my last goodbye and I'm so thankful for that. To me, our day was the sweetest goodbye you can ever have and the best gift she ever gave me. Strangely, life has been pleasantly kind to me by way of goodbyes.

● ● ● ● ●

Two days before he died, Kenny called me. Kenny never called me. In fact, the last time we spoke he specifically told me not to call. I believe his exact words were, "I hate you. You broke my heart. I don't ever want to talk to you again. Leave me alone!" Sounds mean, but if you had known Kenny, you'd understand.

Kenny was simple and kind. Unlike most teens, he had an unshakeable confidence. Consequently, he never pretended to like things just for the sake of fitting in. "I am who I am," he told me on our first date. "I like honey crisp. I like Tootsie Rolls. I don't like coffee." Though his palate was that of a child's, his simplicity likened him to an old man set in his ways. If Kenny ate a salad, it had to be without dressing. If he wore a red shirt, it was with red shoes. If it were Wednesday, he'd watch Sports Center. When we first started dating, this is what I enjoyed most about Kenny, his unapologetic openness.

That all changed after we broke up, and his transparency now included his disdain for me. Clearly, Kenny hadn't meant what he had said. It was his broken heart talking. We've all been there, said and done things in the heat of the moment just to lash out. I myself would eventually get there, three years later, when I broke up with Gums. Kenny needed to be angry with me, so I did my best to give him space, hoping one day he'd feel differently.

His call came while on a long, slow train ride back to New York City. I had spent the weekend in Boston partying with my two older brothers. Sounds harmless, and it was, that is, until we were running for our lives. All things considered, it was one of the best weekends of my life.

Michael had started grad school at MIT earlier that fall. Intent on having a sibling weekend, Brian and I traveled from our respective universities to visit our big brother. Finally, despite of our age differences, we had all finally arrived at the same place in life, as poor college students ready to blow off steam and partake in some shenanigans.

Though, for me the weekend offered much more than an opportunity to party, it would be our first time socializing together as peers. After that weekend, I had hoped to show Michael and Brian that I was no longer their baby sister, but rather, their younger, smarter, prettier, more talented sister. Hold your applause.

Should we all be together, my brothers and I will still sit around and reminisce about the events that transpired that weekend. "Hey, Michael, remember that one time you almost got us killed?" I'll say. The mere mention of it makes him cringe every time, which is exactly why I bring it up. I relish seeing that look upon his face, ergo, it is a story I love to tell and tell often. For it was the first time my big brother was not my big brother, but a person—a drunken person. It was a side of him I had never seen before. He took on this whole other personality, funny and carefree, not at all like my big brother. Michael didn't get out-of-control drunk. Michael was studious. Michael was serious. He was responsible.

However, there is nothing responsible about getting wasted and blindly leading your younger siblings into a blizzard. The weather forecast said heavy snowfall and as we later discovered, this was an accurate prediction. After hours of partying with MIT grad students, we stepped outside to find the snow was already stacked thigh-high. Thus we began the slow journey back, the drunkie, the deafie, and me (whose emotional handicaps are too extensive to affix with an -ie).

"Are you sure this is the right way?" I asked Michael.

"Uh… yeah… this way," he pointed.

"We just came from there!" I squealed.

"Right… that way!"

"Ever heard of the Donner Party?" I asked.

We were clearly walking around in circles. Under normal circumstances, I would have asked for directions. Alas, it was a blizzard and my brothers and I were the only ones wandering about outside, as every other intelligent life form had enough sense to stay indoors. So we walked and kept walking for what felt like hours.

While we were walking, I turned to see a plow approaching Brian from behind. In an attempt to warn him, I yelled,

"B-R-I!" only to remember, fuck, he's deaf. I tried to run towards him and get his attention, but the snow was too high. Thankfully, the plow turned the corner of a hidden street. False alarm.

Eventually, we did find our way back to Michael's apartment, alive and mostly sober. In reality, our odyssey only took about forty minutes, yet to be fair, it should have taken five.

"I'm so happy we didn't die," I sighed, untying my scarf.

"Death by snowplow is not what I want inscribed on my tombstone," said Brian.

"Please don't tell Dad," Michael pleaded.

"Like he'd believe me," I grinned, before adding, "aside from almost dying, that was really fun. Thanks, Michael." I had to take full advantage of the situation. When would I get an opportunity such as this again?

The details of that weekend are still so vivid. What we wore, what we drank, what we said, the train; everything from that weekend has been well preserved. It's the last happy memory I have before Kenny died and things went numb. My next happy memory wouldn't come for another year.

As I sat on the train, reviewing all the highlights from the weekend, my phone rang—Kenny. We hadn't spoken in months. Had he even called me for my birthday? I couldn't remember. No matter, he was calling now. Seeing his name flash on my caller ID, confused as well as excited me. It took two rings before I picked up. "Hello?"

The conversation was pretty standard for new exes, forced and awkward. I made the obligatory chitchat and asked about school, work, and family. Still bitter, he responded with one-word answers: good, busy, the same. It didn't bother me; I was happy just to be talking again.

Toward the end of the conversation, Kenny's walls came down a bit. Without having to pry, he started to offer up bits of information, like how he was saving up to buy a house. The conversation started to flow naturally and at one point, I think he actually laughed. Getting ahead of myself, I flashed forward to next summer, envisioning my return to Sacramento. We'd get ice cream at Coldstone. Everything would be okay. I smiled, knowing we had taken a first step towards friendship.

Before we could finish our conversation, the train went through a tunnel. I lost service and of course, my phone died. Like an idiot, I had forgotten my charger back in New York. Typical. I had meant to call him when I got home, but it was late and instead I went to bed. Two days later my phone rang. Unwilling to believe the news, I called him. It went straight to voicemail. In that moment, I knew it to be true—Kenny was dead.

There were no last words, no goodbyes, just a random phone call, between two old lovers trying to become friends.

numb

Part I - Going Numb

"Relationships always end in either one of two ways; you break up or someone dies." Those are words of wisdom that an old boss once offered me after a breakup.

At nineteen, as a sophomore in college, I accepted there would be breakups. What I wasn't prepared for was a third option, you break up and then someone dies. To be fair, this usually doesn't happen until you're at least fifty, or so I thought.

At some point in life, you get a phone call that everyone dreads, one that in turn, makes telemarketers look like a blessing. In January 2005, I received such a phone call. "Kenny's dead." Amazing. Two words can change your whole life.

Kenny and I dated from my senior year of high school through my freshman year of college. He was the person who trained me to use the register when I started working at Best Buy, my first job. "He's hot!" my friend said when she met him. "Looks like a black Heath Ledger." Though at first the thought struck me as odd, I eventually agreed. "Yeah, a lanky, black Heath Ledger, minus the sexy Australian accent."

When we first started going out, I figured Kenny would be a rebound from my first boyfriend, Sean. As a senior in high school looking to go away for college, a serious boyfriend wasn't at the top of my priorities. Still, there was a sweet boyish charm to Kenny that I found irresistible. Thus, when he surprised me by leaving a red rose and stuffed animal on my car for Valentines Day, I saw it as endearing rather than cliché. In that way, our fling turned into young love.

However, like many kids who go away to college and try to maintain a long-distance relationship, I quickly realized one of the many reasons why it doesn't work. People change. More specifically, I had changed. Suddenly, our mutual love for cheese fries wasn't enough. Booger fights no longer seemed amusing. Explaining this to Kenny, who refused to accept we were no longer right for each other, was one of the hardest things I've ever done. Hurting the people you love is never easy. I'll never forget the look of anger on his face as he sped away in his new blue Mustang convertible, the car that would eventually become his grave. That June was the last time I saw him alive. Six months later, I was at his wake.

It goes without saying, going to your recent ex-boyfriend's wake is traumatizing. Perhaps even more traumatizing is going to your ex's wake and unwittingly telling his new girlfriend, "You guys were such great friends. He cared so much about you (as a friend)," because no one bothered to mention that they had started dating. And why would I assume he had moved on? After all, he was still telling me how much he loved me, how he couldn't possibly love another. Four or five subtle hints later, like the story of their first kiss, I eventually figured out the true nature of their relationship. To say I felt uncomfortable is an understatement. I'm lucky that Kari, being the kindhearted graceful girl that she is, didn't outright slap me. Things couldn't have gone worse, or so I thought. Worse than going to your ex's funeral and belittling his new girlfriend is having his grandma repeatedly call you the love of his life in front of his new girlfriend, a girl you just insulted yet now must comfort. The day was brutal but not nearly over.

After the wake, my mom and I went out to lunch at a restaurant near our house. Now back in California, I couldn't wait to eat some authentic Mexican food, something warm, saucy, and covered with cheese. Since Kenny's death my once-ferocious appetite had become scarce. If anything could recover my hunger, it would be a chicken enchilada. My eyes were still sore and puffy from bawling that I could hardly read the menu.

Not two seconds after placing our order, my mom asked, "Why do you hate me?"

I stared at her, thinking, ARE YOU OUT OF YOUR MIND? You want to do this NOW? My reply was, "Well, I'm really hungry. How about you?"

This was one of the reasons I hated her. Everything was always about her, my ex-boyfriend's funeral being no exception. Nevertheless, I had no intention of ever telling her this or getting into a confrontation, especially after Kenny's wake. I was content on passively hating her and pushing her away, a skill at which I had become quite adept over the past year.

Using college as my means for escape, I fled across the country to New York. During school breaks, I'd fly home to Sacramento and rather than stay with my mom, I'd crash with Soraya or my on-and-off-again boyfriend Sean.

Refusing to drop the subject, my mom repeated, "I want to know why you hate me. What have I ever done to you?"

"I don't want to talk about this," I sighed. Classic Mom.

"I'm your mother. I have a right to know."

Typically, when it comes to confrontations with my mom and given the choice of fight or flight, I choose flight. Be the bigger person, Ali. Walk away, I'll tell myself from high atop my pedestal. It's not worth the hassle. She's not ready to hear what you have to say. But there comes a time, when even those who fly must fight.

"Fine," I told her. "I feel like you haven't been a mother to me. You care more about the men in your life than you do about us. 'Cause you left us alone for a week without anything, not even a car, just a few dollars for groceries, so you could go on a trip with your new boyfriend. I was thirteen. You never take responsibility for anything. If it weren't for me, Monika and Kyle would do whatever they wanted. You always make me feel bad for not spending more time with you, so I cancel my plans, go out to dinner with you, and what do you do? You spend the whole time outside having a smoke or on the phone. You don't really want to spend time with me. You're never around. You weren't there for my first prom, my first anything. Oh, and by the way, moms aren't supposed to wear clothes from Forever 21, because it's for twenty-one-year-olds. Grow up."

When it was all over, I felt empty. She was right. I needed to tell her. Anger was so much more rewarding than sadness. Finally, thoughts of Kenny no longer plagued my mind. This, I'm sure, is what my mom was really aiming for all along, a way to distract me from my misery. Mission accomplished. Thank you.

Afterwards I thought, there, I said it! Can we please move on now?

She hadn't expected me to respond, not like that at least. Rarely when people ask you a direct question do they want an honest response. When it comes to my mom, the case is never. I waited for her to say something, but she gave me nothing. She remained quiet. Our food came and we sat there silently, watching it get cold.

The next day, there was an envelope addressed to me on my mom's dining room table. Inside lay a thirteen-page handwritten letter, single-spaced, written on the front and back. I've only read the letter once, but I remember it well.

The gist of it: of course I didn't understand. How could I? I was still too young to sympathize with how hard her life has been. Until I walk a mile in her shoes (her words, not mine), I won't be able to conceive the decisions she's had to make. Hopefully, in the future, I'll realize what she did was for the best. Rather than be selfish, I should be more grateful to her, the world's most loving mother. I was being hypercritical and dramatic. I needed to change. Clearly, I am the one with the problem. Not her.

In her spare time, my mother writes romance novels. Though she has never gotten published, judging from her letter, she clearly has the talent to paint a dramatic picture. For in only thirteen pages, she managed to capture every gut-wrenching human emotion. Bravo.

When I was done reading, I folded the letter back up and went to the kitchen to make myself a peanut butter and jelly sandwich. My mom is so thoughtful, I thought, laughing to myself. She knows how hard this is for me, and that's why she keeps picking stupid arguments. She's trying to help me!

The next day I received another phone call: "AJ killed himself."

AJ was a family friend. During junior high and high school, he acted like an older brother to me, always looking out and threatening to beat up anyone who bothered me. My junior year, AJ got kicked out of school for dealing drugs, which earned him a reputation as a real "bad boy." As things in life often go, he and I lost touch. I had heard through friends he had a daughter and was using hard drugs.

Depressed over custody issues and high on meth, he hung himself in his parents' house. His little sister found him.

Generally, when a friend calls and says someone we know has just committed suicide, my initial reaction is not to thank her for calling, as if she had simply bailed on our weekly Tuesday dinner. However, I had reached my limit in terms of emotional trauma.

I returned to New York a few days later. Too proud to reach out to friends or family, I found a therapist at school and started receiving grief counseling.

Part II- Fates Worse Than Death

Grief sucks because it's not funny. There is nothing entertaining about grief, unless it's an indie movie about someone else's life. Even then, it can suck. As a person who avidly believes laughter cures all, I found the worst part of grief was the absence of laughter. I no longer understood how to be light. Grief was not an overwhelming feeling of sadness. It was a pervading numbness. I was void of any emotion. Nevertheless, I smiled on cue, laughed after every joke. I remembered what happiness looked like and acted accordingly.

If the grieving process were a class, I would have gotten an "A." Always an overachiever, I excelled at coping methods. I became so knowledgeable about grief that I could have easily written a self-help book: Say Goodbye to Grief: 3 Easy Steps to Accepting Your Loss. Then, when it'd take off and become a bestseller, I would have the voice from Moviefone narrate my book on tape. Step one: see a therapist. Step two: read about the grief cycle and its five phases—denial, anger, bargaining, depression, and acceptance. Step three: get enough sleep, eat well and exercise. Also recommended: surround yourself with activities, friends, and write about your experiences. Check, check, and check.

I waited, but despite my proactive efforts, nothing changed. For the first time in my life I felt broken which in turn, made me feel bitter. It's one thing to sit around and sulk, but I was actually trying to get better and getting nowhere. "Time," everyone said, "time heals all wounds." Bullshit, I thought.

The summer after Kenny's death, I returned to Sacramento and moved in with Sean. He was my first boyfriend and first love. Like Kenny, Sean was extremely handsome. He looked like Pharrell Williams from N.E.R.D., who became my ideal guy in high school after seeing the video for Rock Star. More importantly, Sean was one of the only people I knew whose family was more fucked up than mine. At the time, it offered me a sense of comfort, knowing somebody else's life was shittier. Not to mention, it gave us something in common, helping us to form a bond that we naively mistook as true love.

After Kenny died I told Sean, "Look, we need to talk," five words that never fail to strike fear in the hearts of men. I imagined him on the other side of the phone, wincing as he braced himself for what came next, "I can't do this anymore. Either you want to be together or you don't. I can't do this in-between shit with you."

"Okay."

"Okay, yes or okay, no?"

"Okay, yes."

The relationship was a mess. We fought constantly. Not surprisingly, our sex life sucked. For one, we never had any. This was his decision, not mine. There was always some excuse: I'm tired, I'm not in the mood, I'm busy.

Just to make sure it wasn't me, I grabbed my boobs and ass; yep, still there. He's cheating, I concluded, which seemed completely rational at the time.

Consequently, I began checking his phone for scandalous text messages, especially ones from Brittany. That bitch always had a thing for Sean and hated me for it. Yes, I became that girl.

To justify my actions, I'd tell myself he couldn't be trusted. "Why do you have to keep in touch with people you slept with?" or "Why are they texting you at one in the morning?"

I searched and searched his texts, but none of them ever validated my suspicions.

Poor Sean got so frustrated that he offered to see a couples therapist. "Couples therapy? Are you crazy? We're twenty. We're not married. We're not going to therapy," I told him. Meanwhile, I'd quietly cry myself to sleep as I lay next to him every night.

Despite everything, I stayed. I had nowhere else to go and under no circumstances was I willing to live with my mom. I'm still not sure why Sean didn't leave me. It's not easy being in a relationship with a depressed person, so I give him credit for trying. Most likely it was out of guilt. He didn't want to be the guy who dumped the depressed girl. Or perhaps he felt obligated to take care of me, since I clearly couldn't do that myself. Somehow, we managed to make it through the summer. Come August, I returned to school in New York.

Back in 2005, when I was a junior in college, MySpace was the place where wannabe musicians networked and little girls posted pictures of themselves in a certain pose that coined the term "boob shot." But for me, MySpace was where I first discovered my little sister was depressed.

After "casually" checking Sean's page, I clicked on my sister's profile, where I found pictures of Monika's arms and legs, scored like a tic-tac-toe game. The cuts were so wide; it looked like she had drawn on her skin with lipstick. Digital cameras were still so pixilated back then that I couldn't be sure it wasn't. Monika was only fourteen; it was normal for girls her age to start experimenting with makeup. "Please be lipstick. Please be lipstick," I prayed as I called my mom to tell her what I had found. After seeing the pictures online, my mom told me she was going to speak to Monika. Later that night she called back; the cuts were real.

"I'm going to call around and find her a therapist," my mother assured me.

Effectually, I spent the whole fall semester counting down the days until Christmas, when I would fly back to Sacramento. Ironically, that was the same year a friend introduced me to Advent calendars. However, unlike my friend's calendar, which was filled with chocolate, my days were filled with anxiety.

That Christmas I returned to Sacramento to discover Monika was still not receiving help. Though she wasn't seeing a psychiatrist, my sister did inform me that she had started to see demons. Even more unnerving was the way she said it. For I imagined that the way a person reacts to seeing a demon was similar to what I watched on cartoons growing up. By all accounts my sister should have been terrified and although she said she was afraid, her voice was monotone. Nothing in her face expressed any sort of reaction. She didn't even look at me as she said it. Instead she kept her eyes fixed ahead of her as she sat hunched over in the recliner. She may have responded to my questions, but I could see that nothing I did or said was registering. She was catatonic.

When I asked my mom why Monika still wasn't seeing anyone, she blamed it on bureaucracy. None of the psychiatrists under her plan were taking new patients. While this may have been true, it made me wonder, what exactly did my mom consider an emergency? Certainly not demons, that was for sure.

Reading my look of disapproval, my mother cried, "I'm not strong enough, Ali. Do you know how hard this is for me? How do you think this makes me feel? I can't. I can't." With that she bowed her head, threw up her hands and shook them as if gesturing don't look at me, before retreating to the garage.

My mother's concept of dealing with problems, may it be parenting or just a hard day, is having a smoke in the garage. There she'll stay until she's finished the entire pack, essentially hotboxing the garage as she stares silently at boxes of our childhood trinkets.

I had no idea how to help my sister either. I was a twenty-year-old college student. Sure, I was an RA, but for the most part my job entailed mediating roommate fights over dirty dishes or baking cookies for Grey's Anatomy viewing parties. If a resident had any real problems, I was trained to direct them to campus resources or give them pamphlets. Though they've always seemed lame to me, at the time I was so lost, I would have given anything for a pamphlet.

Unsure what to do, I called Sean. Over the years, Sean and I had gone through so much together that Monika was like a sister to him. It was he who suggested I take her to the psychiatric clinic around the corner from where he worked. Had he worked at a veterinary hospital, I would have happily taken her there too. Anything was better than my mom's house.

My sister's room smelled like a homeless person was squatting in it. Not a single inch of floor was visible under the carpet of garbage, dirty clothes, old food, and random broken objects. Clearly, my mother had never been in Monika's room. If she had, she would have easily seen the half-empty box of condoms on Monika's dresser.

With a large garbage bag in hand, I began to sort through everything. Imagine dumpster diving in the comfort of your own home. The amount of trash from food alone was overwhelming: 7-Eleven slushies, fast food wrappers, chip bags, and candy, all half-eaten and probably weeks old. Like a squirrel preparing for winter, I found that my sister had balled up and stashed her dirty underwear into small dark corners, some with used bloodied pads still attached. Worst of all were the hundreds of safety pins scattered everywhere, which she obviously didn't use for sewing.

After a while, I didn't even bother looking. I just started shoving whatever I could grab into the trash, telling myself it was good practice. I've always wanted to be on a game show, particularly the kind where the challenge is to grab as much cash as you can as the wind tunnel swirls it around you. Hours later, when the floor was once again visible, there were three giant industrial garbage bags filled with my sister's depression.

At the clinic the doctors examined Monika and declared her a danger to herself. "Your sister is severely depressed and slightly psychotic. She admitted to wanting to kill herself. So, legally, we were obligated to admit her for a week. We suspect she's bipolar," the doctor explained. Afterwards they sent me home to collect clothes for Monika. According to the list, she wasn't allowed to have shoelaces, drawstrings, jewelry, or even wire in her bra, things I had never considered potential threats. Then again, I don't consider a candlestick to be particularly menacing either, but according to the board game Clue, it's a murder weapon. I suppose when you're desperate, anything will do.

While Monika was in the hospital, my extended family reached out. They asked, of course, "Why is Monika so depressed? What happened?" What could I tell them? I hardly understood it myself. At a loss for words, I could only say, "I don't know."

"Well, how can we help? Do you need anything for her room? I was thinking of sending a lamp but I didn't know what color she'd like…" my cousin said, and I could hear through the phone, she was desperate to help.

"Sure that'd be great," I told her. "Make it purple."

Giving Monika's room a makeover was Soraya's mom's idea. "It'd be nice to give her a fresh start when she comes out," Kelly said. Soraya's family has always been like a surrogate family to me. Kelly took me shopping and paid for everything: bright pillows of different fluffy textures, a rainbow comforter, lime sheets, and lavender curtains. Kelly kept filling the cart with items. Her kindness overwhelmed me. Kelly wasn't my mom, and yet she was more of a mother to me than my own.

When Monika came home a week later depressed and medicated, I waited for her to say something about the room but she didn't. Instead she marched angrily up to my mother and I, demanding to know where her clothes were.

"Ali threw them away," my mom replied before exiting to the garage.

This was not entirely true. Monika's clothes were hidden in the garage. Most of them, anyway. While cleaning out her room, I took the liberty of sorting through her closet and throwing away anything that had more than five holes, chains, and crossbones. Still, I was willing to let her believe my mom and take the blame, so I told her, "The doctor said you're not allowed to wear black or clothes that cover your body. I'm just doing what he told me."

"You had no right to do that!" she screamed, storming away to her room.

I followed her and watched as she picked up a long thick bike chain, which she began swinging around her head like a whip. Trying to reason with her, I told her to put down the chain and talk to me. Not long after, I realized my mistake—attempting to use reason when dealing with a person who's swinging around a chain is pointless.

Throwing the chain to the floor, she pushed past me and charged for the bathroom. I tried to block her, but despite our five-year age difference, Monika has always been bigger, heavier, and stronger than me. I would have had an easier time stopping a linebacker. Luckily, I was able to wedge my foot in the door, leaving just enough space for me to wiggle through.

Monika yelled at me to get out, but I refused. That's when she grabbed my throat and started to squeeze. Though she didn't entirely cut off my air supply, I didn't find it to be a comfortable position either. It shocked me, really. My sister had never been a violent person, so this was the last thing I expected. Yet even stranger was that as she held my neck, she apologized: "I'm sorry, I don't want to hurt you. Please leave." A few seconds later, she loosened her grip and I left.

I walked to the living room to find Kyle on the couch, watching TV, and my mom still smoking in the garage. When I told my mother what had happened, she said, "Your sister is very sick, Ali, give her some space. Try not to fight with her."

●●●●●

Part III- Everything Ends

Winter break ended a week later, forcing me to return to New York and leave my sister. Back in the city, time crept along. The one-year anniversary of Kenny's death came and went. A year of my life had gone by. The closest thing to acceptance that I got was accepting that life pretty much sucked. In fact, things had gotten worse. However, when a person hits rock bottom, he or she has nowhere to go but up. This was the pep talk I gave myself each morning as I got out of bed.

Then late that March, I went to a friend's birthday party and to my surprise, enjoyed myself. As monumental as the moment was for me, nothing particularly extraordinary happened. I smiled, and that smile was followed by a laugh, a genuine guttural laugh. Each day after that got a little easier, since being happy didn't seem like such a chore.

To be sure, nothing about my situation had improved. Kenny was still dead. After the hospital, my sister started seeing a therapist regularly and taking medication. Even so, Monika continued to act out and put herself in danger. The only thing I had going for me was that I gathered enough sense to break up with Sean. It sounds cruel to say, after all we went through together, but ending a destructive relationship was for the best. A few months after we had broken up, I found out that he actually did cheat on me. By that point it didn't matter, but it provided some comfort knowing I wasn't entirely crazy. While things were still by no means perfect, I finally believed they could and would change.

That December I wanted nothing more than to curl up in a ball and ignore the world. Seeing Monika so sick made me feel weak and helpless. If anything, my actions were motivated by fear of losing someone else I loved. She was my reason to fight, to get better. Sometimes that's all we need: a reason to be better than we are.

the importance of being modest

In getting my heart broken, I learned that the process of falling in love is much like falling out of love; both require playing a game of six degrees of separation with your lover. When my best friend, Soraya, started dating her boyfriend every other word out of her mouth was Ehssan, as if she had Tourette's syndrome and couldn't control herself. After my tenth eye roll, she finally got the hint and attempted to stifle her excitement, yet to no avail; everything was a potential trigger waiting to be set off. I yawned and this sent her squealing with laughter.

"What?" I barked in irritation.

"You yawned. When Ehssan yawns, it's so cute. His eyes tear up..." and her voice trailed off. Then she made that pouty face people get when looking at an adorable puppy, her brows furrowed, eyes drooped, probably picturing his stupid face, yawning. Had I not been driving I would have punched her stupid face.

Honestly, I should have been more sympathetic, considering she's listened to my twitterpated rants more times than I care to remember. More importantly, she has stood by me through my heartaches. I'm not sure who was hurt more by my breakup, me or my poor friends who were forced to endure my "I'm through!" speech time and time again. Each version was slightly different than the last, though they all essentially ended the same: "I mean it this time. We're over!"

Whether I was trying to convince them or myself, I'm not sure. Though one thing is certain. No one bought it, myself included. Nor could I blame them. Any time you have to qualify a statement with, "I mean it this time," chances are you're not going to follow through. When it came to Gums there was always a next time, and I'd be right back where I started, reciting my well-rehearsed goodbye speech. I wish I could give my friends those two years back, but I'm no magician.

By far, the worst part of a breakup is the relics: sentimental trinkets, landmarks, memories, or routines, all of which haunt you well after the relationship ends. Pictures, gifts, or leave-behinds are easy to dispose of—you return them, burn them, or box them up so they're out of sight. But then there are the things you can't control or account for, such as a song. It's not necessarily your song, just a song that reminds you of him, and all of a sudden you're crying in a public place, again; this time it's Barnes & Noble. Afterwards I decided it was in fact acceptable to wear sunglasses at night and indoors. Sunglasses became my best friend; mascara, my enemy.

the importance of being modest

Years later Gums told me what haunted him most was turning on the light. "I can't even look at a light switch, Ali," he confided to me. "Close da' lights," was our inside joke, a way of poking fun at my fobby immigrant family. We'd say it every night before going to bed, then fall asleep laughing in each other's arms. Now this mundane object confronted him everywhere. It was another bittersweet reminder of things lost.

As for me, I didn't need a light switch to remind me of our breakup. Gums' career was burgeoning, making him annoyingly unavoidable. Everyone fantasizes about dating a celebrity, yet few consider the inevitable and formidable breakup. I hadn't seen him in weeks and somehow I couldn't escape him. As fate's sardonic humor would have it, I saw him more now that we were broken up than when we dated. His face and name were everywhere, in the paper, online, when I stepped onto the street, on an airplane.

Unwittingly, I opened up my roommate's magazine to see his picture. It was a short interview. Only one line referenced our breakup and while my name wasn't mentioned, it was enough to send me into a tailspin. I threw the magazine across the room screaming, and cried. There it was in print for me and everyone else to read. Our breakup, my heartache.

His success was a personal attack. He didn't have to read about me or stumble upon my picture. He didn't have to overhear conversations in passing about how great and talented I am. His friends didn't ask him, "Hey, how's Ali's teaching career going? Is she coming out with any new lessons?" I, on the other hand, was subjected to this and more as for some reason, people think that just because you've dated a celebrity, the usual breakup rules don't apply. Sure, I love talking about my breakup. No, please, go ahead, ask me more prying questions. I know, isn't the guy who broke my heart so talented! With each compliment, my already shattered heart became a little more bitter and jaded.

To avoid future meltdowns, I started boycotting our favorite shows and anything associated with comedy because it reminded me too much of him. Then, hoping to cheer me up, my girlfriend forced me to make a list of Things Gums Ruined: Korean fried chicken, osso bucco, the chicken and rice cart on 66th and 6th, the 7 train, Ratatouille, WALL-E, soup, Uniqlo, Dunkin' Donuts, Long Island City, the Village. Mostly the list consisted of food and places where we ate food. Conversely, we created another list—Things You Can Do Without Gums: eat carbs! Again, this list consisted of mostly food.

Holidays too became a time for mourning. Each one seemed to carry some sentimental memory of him, even Mother's Day, which we spent with my mom's family in Jersey. Come each holiday, all I could think was, this time last year Gums and I were… and now… now we're nothing. No matter how happy I was to be with family, holidays reminded me of my breakup.

the importance of being modest

Our first Christmas together, Gums took me out to an expensive dinner in New York. Knowing I was a huge fan of the show Top Chef, he surprised me with a dinner at Tom Colicchio's restaurant, Craft Steak. There he handed me a red and black shiny box with a pearl white satin ribbon tied around it. Right away I recognized it to be jewelry, since that's what I asked for. Earlier that month he asked me what I wanted for Christmas and my birthday to which I unabashedly replied, jewelry. When he asked me again a week later, hoping I had changed my mind, I reiterated my previous statement, "I—WANT—JEWELRY! I'm not asking you for a ring, silly. Just get me a charm bracelet or something."

Jewelry is what I require from all my boyfriends our first Christmas together, a sort of test as to how well they know me. The year before, the Muslim RA gave me a set of painted glass jewelry. I loved it. Having extremely similar tastes, there was no doubt I'd love whatever Gums gave me. A quarter-machine bracelet would have even sufficed. Still, I was curious to see what he'd choose.

Before I could undo the bow, his face beaming with pride, he informed me, "It's from Saks." It was his first time in the store, let alone buying jewelry. "I asked the saleswoman for help," he explained. "She asked what you were like and I said you like things that are classic but with a modern twist. Anyhow, it was very expensive, more than I thought it would be, but then again, you're worth it."

His story confused me. How did he expect me to react? Grateful perhaps, that he had gone to the most expensive store in town and bought me a present? Never being one to be preoccupied with designer brands, I didn't care where it was from. Actually, it made me uncomfortable, knowing the thing I was about to receive probably cost as much as my week's earnings.

Both of us came from working-class families, so part of me understood his sense of pride. Neither of us ever imagined we'd be sitting in such a restaurant, going to such shops, and at such a young age. In that moment, we had everything. Plus, it was sweet how he described my taste to the saleswoman, classic but modern. I hadn't thought about it before, but when he said it I thought, yeah, that's me.

I opened the box to see several grayish imperfect pearls dangling from a silver chain bracelet. It was simple yet stunning. Test passed.

Our last Christmas together was in the winter of 2009. We spent a week with my family in Sacramento. Technically we weren't a couple. In fact, we had been "broken up" for a year. Still, no matter how hard we tried something kept drawing us back together. Denial, perhaps.

"Why don't you come up for my birthday?" I suggested, expecting it'd be just for the weekend. Next thing I knew, he'd booked a plane ticket and hotel room for an entire week. His actions left me speechless. After years of living on crumbs of his time, a week together seemed like a Thanksgiving feast. His overture was the grand gesture I had been waiting for. Years and years of fighting had finally paid off. Gums was ready to commit. I couldn't have asked for a better present, but he gave me another anyway.

Come Christmas day he handed me yet another shiny box, this time containing a red Marc Jacobs wallet quilted with baby lambskin. Unlike the bracelet, it felt impersonal, not to mention, fugly. Nothing about it said classic with a modern twist. If anything, it reminded me of L.A. Like the people, it was a farce—expensive and seemingly beautiful on the outside, but of no real worth. (Don't worry, Los Angelans, I'm not talking about you, but the person next to you who looks exactly like you).

Not wanting to be rude, I managed to say thank you. I even tried to lie and pretend I loved it. However, I've never been good at lying, especially to Gums, who's always seen through me. No, I'm not mad you didn't call. Of course I understand that you're too busy to come to my brother's wedding. I'm happy, really. It's not that I wanted to lie to Gums, but rather, that I wanted to believe what I said. It's just a wallet. It doesn't mean anything. Besides we were having an amazing week, at last. All the same, I couldn't help but wonder, is this how he sees me, or worse, how he wants me to be?

A few months later, on Valentine's Day, Gums flew to New York for Fashion Week. During the day, we went shopping.

Or rather, he shopped and I watched. We went to stores I typically avoid, places where price tags make me cringe and the absence of one induces sheer panic. I'd love to buy this shirt, ma'am, but that would mean not eating for a month, which coincidentally, is probably what it would take for me to fit into this in the first place. I couldn't imagine what would warrant making an item cost this much. Does the dress come with a lifetime warranty that ensures it's always the right size? Can it do magic? Is it made from a rare bird with special healing powers?

As I patiently sat, watching him browse the men's clothes in his new favorite store, Marc Jacobs, he turned to me and said, "Try something on." I did, and looked terrible, like a girl playing dress-up in her daddy's sailor uniform. When I came out of the dressing room the saleswoman asked, "How'd it work out?"

"It didn't fit."

"What size are you?"

"Four."

"Are you sure?" she asked, pausing to scan my body. "Wait here, I have just the dress for you." With a smile she turned and walked away.

Was I sure? WAS I FUCKING SURE? I'm a size four, damn it! How dare she? Several minutes later she returned with a dress that I had seen earlier but passed over, joking to Gums, who would ever wear this? Before I could express my deepest disinterest, I happened to see the tag, size two. Grinning like the Cheshire Cat, I grabbed the garment and happily tried it on. To my surprise, I loved it. Gums did too.

"We'll take it. How much is it?" he asked.

"Twenty-eight hundred," she replied coolly.

I shot him a look of terror, pleading with him not to buy it. It was too much. I shook my head no as if to say, I don't need this dress, really. Seeing my discomfort, he smirked, kissed me, and said, "You deserve a nice dress." Then, hanging his arm around my waist, he pulled me close and kissed me again. It felt too much like we were in the movie Pretty Woman, which would be a romantic thought, if it didn't make me a prostitute.

Standing at the register I saw the wallet he gave me for Christmas, sitting in the display case. "Oh, there's my wallet," I said.

"You mean the one you hate? Do you know how difficult it is to get that wallet?" he asked, shooting me a look.

"Oh, I love that wallet!" the cashier chimed in. "You have good taste," she complimented Gums. "Who's your favorite designer?"

"Marc."

"Mine too!" she squealed. Then she turned to me. "What about you?"

"Um, I dunno…" I stammered. I didn't know any designers in general, let alone off the top of my head.

"She's not really into that stuff," Gums explained as they shared a laugh. He paid, but it was at my expense.

● ● ● ● ●

Not long after, we were broken up again and talking about getting back together—again. Yet, sitting across from him in a restaurant, I could hardly recognize the person in front of me as the man I fell in love with four years ago. His hair was still picked out like when we first met, but so much had changed. I searched for the boy whose arms I had slept in years ago, thanking God that such a person existed, and praying he always would, back when I was too young to know that everything changes, good and bad. Now he sat before me, in a $3,000 leather jacket and a scarf.

"I love this scarf," he declared. "Everyone in L.A. thinks its Dolce and Gabbana when they see it and ask me when I got it, since it looks vintage, but it's just an old knit scarf." His words sounded so foreign. Was he trying to be ironic or impress me? I didn't give a shit about his scarf. I just wanted things to be the same, to sing silly songs like we used to. As I looked at him I knew we could never go back, so why did I still love him?

That's when he told me, "I'm a modest person but I'm not worried about you finding someone better. I mean, I'm pretty amazing! I'm young, successful, I've got money and I don't do drugs."

Before I had a chance to respond, we were interrupted by our waiter, a hipster named Butch who, with his man gruff and plaid shirt, looked like a shrunken version of the Brawny man. The restaurant sat just around the corner from my apartment and offered discounted burgers every Friday, which I took full advantage of, making me a regular. There I'd see Butch, ask about his day job (teaching children's yoga) and make small talk about holiday sweaters. I remember thinking he was short, but sweet. He asked me out once, on a coffee date, except I lost his number. Not that I ever planned on calling. After all, his name was Butch, which ironically is the least sexy name in history.

"I'll have the banana crepe," I told Butch, who smiled as he placed his hand on my back, as if restating his interest.

"Nothing for me," Gums said, focusing on Butch's hand. Despite being hungry, Gums refused to order. Now that he was on camera, Gums took to eating only salads and air, which would have been fine if the kitchen was serving its full menu. It wasn't. I told him to ask if they had any celery sticks lying around. He didn't find this funny. Low blood sugar makes people cranky.

As Butch walked away, Gums grunted, "That guy wants to fuck you."

"Yeah, and...?" I shot back sarcastically, thinking, what does that have to do with anything? So much for thinking I'd never find better.

When my crepe arrived I delightfully dove in. Forking a small piece, I held it up to Gums, who snapped at me, "You know I can't eat that. I'm on a diet." Sighing loudly, I pouted and sank into my chair to overtly display my disappointment. This never failed to make Gums laugh.

Normally, he'd tell me, "You think you're a princess, don't you?" before kissing my forehead, amused by my mini-tantrum. Toward the end of the relationship, I started using it to defuse tense moments or conversations that had no foreseeable resolution. So I waited for him to laugh, but he didn't.

The man I loved no longer existed. For the man I loved was humble and would have known that truly modest people don't need to proclaim their modesty. That man would have seen Gums' statement as I did, as a contradiction of terms. We no longer laughed together, ate together, or lived in the same world. As I saw it, the only thing left to do now was to follow through with the lives we chose.

Part of me always suspected it would end this way. His career would eventually take him to L.A and fame would complicate things. However, like a fool in love, I had to hope we would be the exception and not the rule. The saddest day was realizing that we weren't.

a dead shark

"When you run, make sure you run to something, and not away from, 'cause lies don't need an aeroplane to chase you anywhere." – *The Avett Brothers*

I had my reasons for leaving. Work, for one, was sucking away my soul. There is a reason why twenty-five percent of teachers in New York City quit within their first two years—a statistic I myself narrowly escaped. Regardless of the circumstances, I've always hated quitting. Hence, I often find myself in miserable situations. Yet, even more than quitting, I hate listening to people complain about a situation they refuse to change. Bystanders. I'd been talking about leaving my job for the last three years, since I started teaching. I had become one of *those* people, content to be discontent.

Teaching was my first job out of college. At twenty-one, I was still so green. They always talk about how difficult it is to teach inner-city children, due to the lack of funding, parental support, lower literacy rates, etc. What they never mention, however, are the many psychological challenges that come with teaching at-risk children, and the weight of working in an environment where almost every story is a sad one. These children weren't textbook case studies from my sociology classes, but faces with names and personalities. Each day they came in wearing expressions of anger, pain, and neglect. How could a child who hadn't yet learned to read already know so much suffering?

My only means of survival was hanging onto the small victories, which were few. On the bright side, after my first year, the crying lessened to only every other week. By my third year, I didn't even bat an eye when my administration told me that my sociopathic student, who had just kicked a female student in the face, would be back in my classroom the next day—free of consequences. My growing familiarity and comfort with my surroundings terrified me. I started teaching because I wanted to change the status quo, not accept it. Yet facing the daily reality of my surroundings had soured me. I no longer spoke in a language of solutions, but of problems. If I didn't get out then, I feared I'd never leave.

The final straw came when my principal announced there were more budget cuts and thus, jobs to negotiate. As a special educator, my job was not in jeopardy. Plus with three years in, I was nearly a veteran and no longer at the bottom of the totem pole. At the start of next fall I would receive tenure. Regrettably, others around me would not be so lucky. I looked at the other teachers whose jobs were on the line, people with families, who loved their jobs, and wanted to stay. They deserved to be there next year, not me. So, in the midst of a recession without another job or plan, I told my principal, "I won't be coming back in September." Upon leaving her office, a smile found its way to my face. I instantly felt lighter. It was the sign of a right decision.

Unfortunately, my job wasn't the only thing that had me considering joining a support group. My personal relationships with my mom and with Gums had also reached critical breaking points. I was tired of putting Band-Aids on fractured bones. The feeling reminded me of this scene in Annie Hall. Drawing insight into his relationship with Diane Keaton's character, Woody Allen says, "A relationship, I think, is like a shark, you know? It has to constantly move forward or it dies. And I think what we got on our hands is a dead shark."

Generally, Woody Allen is not someone I consider to be a relationship or life guru but all judgments aside, the man had a point. My life was a shark that had stopped moving forward. Unless something changed, I was going to be a dead shark.

Change was going to be impossible in New York; my life there was too comfortable and my complacency grew by the day. Inside me, though, was this hunger for renewal. I craved space away from everyone and everything familiar. As much as I loved New York, I knew I had to leave.

Telling your parents you want to move across the ocean to a foreign country because you have a "gut feeling" usually provokes one of two questions: "Are you in some sort of trouble?" or, "Is it drugs?" Both reactions are completely understandable. Were a loved one to tell me they wanted to move to Antarctica to seriously pursue ice fishing, based on some "feeling," I'd most likely ask them, "Are you sure that feeling isn't gas or something you ate? How can you be sure this won't pass?" It's all just too intangible.

Hearing a couple say they "just knew" makes me want to vomit. Nothing is more frustrating than being subjected to their lies. You didn't just know. You know now and are parlaying your current knowledge onto the past. Or, more likely, they still don't know and are desperately trying to convince themselves that they made the right decision. With the exception of the late tele-psychic Miss Cleo, no one can ever be sure. Really, there is little difference between couples that "just knew" and the crazies on the subway preaching the apocalypse of raining rabbits; both claim to know something based on a feeling. Their testimonials are just another means of separation, an equivalent to the middle-school taunt, "I know something you don't know." I wanted no part of it.

Yet there I was, sitting in my parents' living room, serving up a huge plate of piping hot hypocrisy. I wanted to give my dad and Julie a better explanation, more than an "I just know," but I didn't have one. As an adult, I didn't need their permission; all the same, I sought their approval. Whether they trust me or simply recognized I was on the verge of a breakdown isn't clear. Nevertheless, they encouraged my move.

Truth is, I've wanted to live in Spain from the moment I first arrived, three years ago, on my first backpacking trip through Europe. There I got this overwhelming gut feeling that said, you belong here. It was the same feeling that brought me to New York and NYU all those years ago, the same feeling I got when I first locked eyes with Gums. It was an instinct that demanded to be heard. Now, that familiar itch was tingling once more, telling me to move to Spain.

When asked my reasons for moving to Spain, I told people I wanted a change of pace, time to do some writing and traveling. In actuality, these were large motivating factors for my move. After reading The Happiness Project by Gretchen Rubin, a book my friend Patty lent to me, I questioned what I really wanted to do with my life. On principle, I tend to avoid books of this genre, self-help books that reek of "I am a middle-aged woman unhappy with my life and searching for meaning." They remind me too much of my mother, the very last person I wanted to emulate. Nevertheless, I read the book and to my surprise, loved it.

While the book didn't tell me anything I didn't already know, it did remind me of several common-sense things you tend to forget as an adult. For instance, whatever you enjoy doing in your spare time is likely your true passion, and therefore, what you should be doing for a living. When I really thought about it, my spare time was dedicated to cooking and writing, yet here I was, a teacher studying for the LSATs. Clearly, something had gone terribly wrong.

As children, we're given mixed signals: follow your dreams, or make money. If you're lucky, the two go hand in hand, like all those little boys who lie in bed fantasizing about one day closing a huge business merger. For the rest of us, we're taught that dreams and financial stability are diametrically opposed. A realist, I accepted the fact that there is no way to make money as a writer, so why even try? Thus, I settled on law school rather than writing. Plus, there was the added blessing of student loans to sort out, another fun detail they leave out when telling bedtime stories about chasing your dreams. I had to become a lawyer because I had to pay off school.

Frustrated yet again with my LSAT homework, I randomly opened up The Happiness Project, hoping to find some inspiration. The passage I landed on read, more or less, Despite clerking for the Supreme Court, I decided not to become a lawyer. For what I truly loved to do is write. Not quite the motivational push I was looking for. Apparently, in addition to my gut, books were also now demanding I give up law to become a writer. Message received, universe, thank you. Should I become a poor writer who never makes it, I figured at the very least I could write a nasty letter to Mrs. Rubin.

Spain would be the antithesis to my life in New York and quite frankly, I welcomed the change. The high-paced living of the city had finally caught up to me. Life in New York never seemed to slow down. I craved to know boredom. This wouldn't be a problem in Spain, considering I still hadn't found a job. That's another thing parents love to hear: "I don't have a job yet; however, I do have a good feeling that it's all going to work out. Trust me."

Earlier that spring, I applied for an assistant teaching program in Spain. While the program practically paid in Skittles, it did offer a visa and lots of free time to spend writing, since I'd only be working twelve hours a week. Indeed, it would've been an ideal opportunity had I not been waitlisted. Not realizing the program was first-come, first-served, I applied late and was forced to play the waiting game. All I could do was be patient and hope for the best, as if that ever worked. In the meantime I applied for other jobs and programs, none of which proved to be fruitful. By the time June rolled around it became evident that I was not getting into the program. I was not going to get a visa. I was not going to have my shot at an amazing adventure where I eat lots of delicious food, find myself, and write about it.

Undeterred, I bought a ticket to Europe. Job or no job, I was intent on moving to Spain, even if it required becoming an illegal alien and busing tables. No work was too base if it meant fulfilling my goal. For whatever misery awaited me in Spain, it could not compare to the misery of my current situation in New York. With all the uncertainty, I should have been afraid. But the voice inside me quelled my fears. As I looked into the face of the Asian woman doing my nails, it occurred to me, I might be you in a few months. Though even that possibility wasn't terrible; at the very least I knew there'd be a happy ending.

Upon telling people my plans to write and travel in Spain, I quickly recognized my mistake. The universal reply was, "So, you're going to write your own Eat, Pray, Love?" After the hundredth time I wanted to gorge my eyeballs out with a dull spork and scream, "Elizabeth Gilbert does not hold a copyright on writing and traveling! The two aren't mutually exclusive to Eat, Pray, Love. Nor is it farfetched that a person who likes to eat and travel would also enjoy writing." Equally annoying were people's pitiable attempts at wit: "So, your book would be like, Eat, Fuck, Eat? Right?"

Their comparisons infuriated me. Even if I did like her book (which was a waste of two days of my life), I wouldn't want to be associated with her experience. I'm sorry, but she divorced her husband, traveled the world, and then proceeded to complain about it for 352 pages. Can you say melodramatic? I'm supposed to want to write my own version of this story? No, thank you. I am nothing like her. If I write a book, it will surely not be about a breakup or heartache.

I have little sympathy for people who feel trapped by the decisions they make. She was right to call herself a criminal jerk for participating in a life she knowingly didn't want. I would never do that. Elizabeth Gilbert was a coward, a woman who couldn't handle her own problems. She ran away. Is it really a surprise that her problems followed her? No matter where she was in the world, she'd end up in the bathroom, crying on the floor, praying. It was so annoying. Not to mention, her selfishness made me want to scream. You're in India, where people have actual problems, you know like, starvation. Find some perspective, please! No one wants to listen to you talk about your feelings and First World problems all the time.

My story has nothing to do with Eat, Pray, Love. Outside of being two women who moved abroad, she and I have absolutely nothing in common. Our stories are quite different, and I intend on keeping it that way.

In early July, before I flew to my brother's wedding in Hawaii, I received an e-mail from the teaching program. Apparently, a new region had opened in Spain and I was no longer on the waitlist. I'd be teaching English at a secondary school in Santiago de Compostela for the coming 2010-11 school year. Overcome with emotion, my knees buckled and I sank to the floor, crying hysterically. Finally, a sign! It's actually all going to work out. I'm going to Spain. Thank you, God. Thank you! As I lay there, on the floor crying and praying to God, it struck me. The lady doth protest too much. Fuck.

little things

During her first week in Spain, while we searched for an apartment together, my roommate caught bedbugs from her hostel. By this point, I had already committed to living with her, which meant it was too late to say, "Thanks, but no thanks. Maybe we can just be friends, or better yet, acquaintances. Not the kind you hang out with but who you chat with occasionally, online." I've never had bedbugs nor did I intend to now that I was in Spain.

It's amazing, the power of suggestion. Just knowing she had bedbugs made me twitch. Then came the mysterious itches. Suddenly, every red spot became suspect. When we walked down the street I tried to maintain a significant lead just so the bedbugs couldn't jump from her to me. Whether or not my tactics worked, I never caught bedbugs. They, however, continued to plague Kathrin for months.

When we first moved into our apartment we washed everything. Can't be too safe, right? Every night I'd hear her toss and turn in the next room, only to see her looking even more drained and sickly in the morning. It was clear she wasn't sleeping. Her pale skin was even paler than usual. Though Kathrin always looked like an Aryan poster child, with her pale skin, blonde hair and blue eyes, now she looked like the Aryan poster child for anemia.

For months this continued. I felt bad. Here she was, a young girl away from home for the first time, far from the normal comforts of her Germany, where the water was sweet and people cared more about education, (her words not mine). She didn't speak the language. She didn't have any friends. What she did have were bedbugs.

Three months after we moved in, Kathrin came to my room, crying hysterically. Her face looked like someone had just killed her cat. "I knew they were biting me! No one believed me but I found one. I found one!" She had caught one of the little buggers. She refused to go into her room and instead stood in our hallway, shaking. "I spray my bed every night before sleep. Then I don't sleep because I feel them! They're biting me! They're biting me."

From what I had heard, bedbugs were microscopic, meaning undetectable to the naked eye. How she managed to see, let alone catch one running across her bed, didn't make sense. Once again, the mere mention made me start to itch, wondering, do I have them too? Funny thing about bedbugs, you can't see them, but that doesn't mean you can't feel them and that they're not there.

little things

The next day, after yet another night of not sleeping, she called an exterminator, who, after a thorough examination declared that bedbugs were not Kathrin's problem. It was nothing. The countless nights of spraying, tossing and turning in her bed and not sleeping, were for nothing. She didn't have bedbugs. She was homesick. Her symptoms were manifestations of a larger problem, problems an exterminator couldn't fix. I'd be lying if I said I haven't experienced the same thing.

En route to our breakup, Gums and I often fought about trivial things, which had nothing to do with our actual problems. We created problems to avoid larger ones. It's easy to inflate, or worse, create problems when you're skirting the truth. Our minds will go to great lengths to protect us from what we're not ready or willing to accept. When we realize we're faced with something we can't fix, we focus on what we can control, something tangible.

After a relationship ends, it's normal for people to ask, what happened? Yet when faced with this question I couldn't help but feel sad and confused. At first, I'd simply tell friends that I didn't know. You'd think I had a reason, being the person who decided to call it quits but I didn't. Instead, I told my friends a story:

It was Election Day and I called Gums to see what he was doing after work. He said he had a show in Brooklyn, close to my house. So I asked him if he wanted to come over afterwards. He said he couldn't. Of course, I got upset and was like, fine do whatever you want then. A few hours later, he called and said he was coming over. So then I got all happy and forgot I was mad in the first place. Typical of him, Gums didn't get there until eleven, which was annoying but whatever, I was happy to see him. I asked him if he voted and he said, "No." I asked him why not and he said, super-defensive, "I was really busy today." Thing is, he's from a swing state, so technically, it could've been a crucial vote.

Whatever, so we're sitting on my couch watching the results from the election, Obama's just climbing and climbing in the polls, and then it's announced. Obama won! So then Gums starts crying and calls his dad saying, "We did it, Dad!" all proud, of um, not voting. Then all of a sudden, he grabs his coat and heads for the door like he's leaving. So I ask him, "You're leaving? You just got here."

And he tells me, "It's just too much right now. I have to go out and celebrate."

And I say, "Why can't you celebrate here with me?"

But he's like, "This is too important, Ali. I have to go." So he leaves and I'm pissed, like, you fucking hypocrite. You didn't even vote, yet here you are crying on my couch, calling your dad, wanting to go out and celebrate? For what? You didn't do shit! So I decided then and there I couldn't do it anymore. I guess it was just the straw that broke the camel's back.

little things

Afterwards, when reality sank in, I knew it wasn't a mistake. So then why the remorse? How was it that two people who loved each other and wanted to be with each other, couldn't make it work? Had I been too quick to break up with him? No, I had been feeling this way for almost a year now. Nothing made sense, including my breakup.

There wasn't a defining reason I broke up with Gums, nor was there a list of reasons. We didn't get into a fight. Things weren't particularly bad. No one cheated. Though, truth be told, a part of me has always secretly wanted an excuse to go crazy, like Angela Bassett in Waiting to Exhale. As much as I wanted to be able to point to something and say, "There, that's the reason we broke up," I couldn't. I just knew I couldn't take anymore.

Figuring out why a relationship doesn't work is a maddening but necessary step in the breakup process. For without the why, there's just this huge question mark looming in the air. Nothing is more paralyzing than the question, could we ever get back together?

The need to know would have driven me insane had a friend not told me, "The road to failure is not made by one bad decision but a series of small ones." At the time we were standing in line at Dunkin' Donuts, where I was ready to buy a donut in spite of proclaiming just minutes earlier that I was going on a diet. Her ploy worked; we walked out of the store sans donut. Still, her words got me thinking. If this was true for donuts, surely it was also true for relationships.

Initially, I blamed his career, as it was the easiest problem to pinpoint. The fall after we started dating, Gums' career took off. On top of writing full-time for an award-winning TV show, he started writing a screenplay. And as much as I wanted to be excited for him, I knew the movie would change things.

Before the movie, Gums and I were inseparable. Whenever I had a particularly bad day at work, which as a first-year teacher was almost every week, I'd go over to his apartment in Queens, close to tears, and be greeted with a huge steak dinner. What can I say? The man knew the way to my heart. Not that I needed all the fuss. Instant ramen would have made me equally content. What really mattered was that he was there for me.

However, with the movie, Gums no longer had time to make steak. All of his free time was spent writing the script, in meetings, or at his actual day job. Consequently, he became the Houdini of boyfriends, always disappearing.

Gums didn't have time to return my calls and when the calls stopped, the fights started. Every time I brought up the subject, he accused me of being unsupportive. He was right. I was being too needy and should have been more patient. After all, he was so accommodating of me when I had a bad day.

Now it was my turn. I needed to be the stronger one. Plus, it wouldn't be like this forever. Just wait.

In order to maximize our time together, I began traveling to Queens after my grad classes in Brooklyn. Although technically part of the same city, any New Yorker will tell you that dating someone in a different borough is practically considered a long-distance relationship. In fact, anyone on a different subway line or involving several transfers is pushing it. However, this wasn't just anyone, it was Gums, the love of my life. He was worth it. This is what I told myself for the first few months that I commuted. And at first, I believed it.

However, come our one-year anniversary that spring, the tiring commute coupled with ignored phone calls and overall neglect fostered feelings of resentment. Clearly, there was only one way to solve this problem: nag. We never spend time together. You don't appreciate everything I do for you. I don't understand why you can't at least send a text, at least something, to let me know you're thinking of me.

We've all seen it and have fallen victim to it—Needy Girl Syndrome.

Nothing is worse than feeling like a needy girl. No one likes that girl, least of all me. Yet the less he gave me the more I needed, and the less inclined he felt to give. Both of us were spiraling away from each other, trying desperately to hold on to what we had. True love, right?

That summer, Gums went upstate to shoot his movie. In spite of popular belief, distance did not make our hearts grow fonder. To the contrary, it emphasized our communication problems. We would often go days without talking. I'd call, but he wouldn't pick up. Then I'd tell myself, don't call. If he wants to talk, he can call! He didn't. Predictably, I'd get angry, and he'd get distant.

Eventually, I decided enough was enough. I needed a call, at least once a day. Period.

"Impossible," he told me without even a second of hesitation.

"What do you mean impossible?" I asked; stretching out the word mean, the way you do when flabbergasted.

"I can't do it," he said calmly.

"As in you're physically incapable? That's ridiculous."

"I'm just not that type of guy."

"What do you mean that type of guy? The type of guy who dials a phone?"

He refused to call. I refused to accept his refusal.

Finally in August he returned from filming, though it was clear things weren't the same between us. The distance had rendered us strangers, strangers who used to be and might still be in love. We were officially in a slump, which, while it sounds like hump, is actually the anti-boner. Our sex life had gone into hibernation. Unable to let go of neither our relationship nor the resentment, we stayed together and fought. We fought in circles, over little things and the same things.

"Can I come over?"

"It's two a.m. Why are you calling me? Are you drunk?"

"Tonight was our premiere party."

"You didn't tell me that…"

"It wasn't a big deal. Don't worry about it. So can I come over?"

"Fine, come over."

A half hour later we were standing at my doorstep fighting.

"It doesn't take a half hour to take a taxi from the Village at this hour. What took you so long?" I barked.

"I got kicked out of the taxi for throwing up. So I had to find another taxi. I left my phone in the first taxi."

"Fine. Come in."

"Are you mad?"

"It's three a.m. I have to get up for work in three hours. We'll talk about this later."

We fought to fight and not for the relationship. Our communication became a competition of who could talk louder. In the end, we would table the argument, since neither of us was willing to back down or listen. Things would get better until our problems resurfaced. Each time, the fracture grew deeper.

Then I broke.

Following the election, I thought back on all the times Gums wasn't there, times when work or an obligation called him away, times like moving into my first apartment, or family birthdays, weddings, graduations, and too many more to count. I wondered what else he'd miss had we stayed together, imagining the birth of our first child, her first steps, dance recitals. He would miss it all, and for what? Money?

Sadly, I already knew what he would say with each absence. Something like, I'm doing this for us, so you don't have to worry about money. Money was a concern; however, so was the amount of time that money demands. I left knowing it would only get worse. He needed work, fame, and money more than he needed me. More than the money, I needed him to be around. Sadly, despite all the little things he missed, I could forgive him for every single one. Except one.

Two months after Gums and I broke up, I received a call from my brother Michael. "Julie's test results came back. It's malignant." Michael's call came on the two-year anniversary of Kenny's death, so it was excellent timing.

It's telling, the people who first come to mind when in a state of shock. For me, that person was Gums, who at the time was premiering his movie at a festival. I called him, but he didn't pick up. So I left him a message saying, "It's an emergency. Call me."

Worried, Gums called me back, "Are you okay? What's happened?" As much as I wanted to tell him, suddenly, I couldn't talk. I just couldn't bring myself to say out loud, my mom has cancer. So I remained silent. "Are you okay? Just tell me if you're okay," he repeated.

"It's Julie. She has cancer," I said.

Gums immediately tried to comfort me. "It's going to be okay. I'll be home Sunday. Call me if you need anything. I love you." Still unable to speak, I said nothing.

By the time he returned from the festival two days later, it was too late. I had gone into an emotional fetal position, blocking out everyone who tried to come close.

I tried to tell him I didn't want to talk but he wouldn't listen. "Ali, I'm begging you! While I was gone I realized you're the one. You're it. And the whole plane ride over, all I could think was, please, please don't crash plane, I need to tell Ali how much I love her. I need to see you."

He kept calling me and telling me how he wanted us to be together, how he needed to see me. I begged him not to push the subject yet his need to discuss his emotions was relentless.

Knowing he wouldn't give up, I told him the one thing that I knew would make him stop, "I don't know if I love you." It worked. He burst into tears and hung up.

Thirty minutes later his mom called. Explaining to your ex-boyfriend's mom that the reason her son is crying is because you told him you didn't love him is truly a fun time. I highly recommend it on days when you're feeling down. Really, it takes your mind off your own problems.

I tried to call him back. No answer. Desperate, I called his friend and asked him to check up on Gums at his apartment. Half-hour later I received a text. Gums was shaken but fine. Emotionally drained, I went to bed.

The next morning, I woke up feeling great. Nothing puts your life into perspective like cancer. My broken heart was now the least of my worries. All those little things suddenly didn't matter. My mom's health was now the only thing I cared about.

In retrospect, it's easy to look back and see the cracks, as the things that were once small and insignificant suddenly become telling and exemplary. Or perhaps we assign meanings to give ourselves validation. I can remember those moments, when I told myself, don't stress the little things. In actuality, it's the little decisions we make that take us to where we are.

Both of us alternated between taking and assigning blame, though it never made a difference. Eventually, after countless unsuccessful reconciliation attempts, therapy, and distance I realized it was never my needs or his job. We were the problem. We didn't know how to communicate. Then again, had we been able to, I'm sure we would have only discovered sooner that we wanted different things from life.

At times it's easy to rationalize that we both got what we wanted and are therefore better off apart. He's in L.A, making money, gaining fame. And I'm in Spain, writing, eating, and traveling.

little things

Still, I think about Gums every day. I even talk about him with my friends. Either from the way I talk about him or by mere intuition they can detect I still love him. I'll admit it, I do. We may be different people now, living separate lives, with little in common, but for some reason unbeknownst to me, I still love him.

Appropriately, they'll ask, "So what happened? Why aren't you two together?" Upon hearing this I'll sigh because I still don't know how to fully explain it, though at least now I understand it. So I settle with, "We just want different things, and I don't see that changing."

Truly, what I want to explain is that I know I'll always love Gums. But knowing this doesn't mean we belong together, are good for one another, and more importantly, that I can't or won't love someone else. My heart isn't so small or weak that it can only hold one person. If anything, my love for him is proof that I am capable of loving someone that much. It's not always easy, but I think of him, and feel hopeful that someday I'll love like that again.

healthy

The day before a group of friends and I flew to Valencia for a festival called Las Fallas, my friend Rachel told me, "I feel like I've been shown how to have a healthy relationship, but I've never had one." It was true; Rachel's parents were one of those rare couples you only hear about in folktales nowadays, the couple still happily married after over twenty years. Despite having loving and functioning parents, Rachel found herself newly out of a relationship, with a person whose destructive behavior was clear to everyone except Rachel.

As Rachel's friend and casual observer, I played my part well and pointed my finger to everything wrong in the relationship. He was controlling, co-dependent, severely depressed—all the red flags you tend to avoid when getting into a relationship and tend to deny once in one. Though Rachel had never had a healthy relationship, her comment made me wonder, had I?

Loving, yes. Unstable, oh definitely. But healthy? What does that even mean? I've never had a lover hit me, if that counts? Mulling it over, I decided it wasn't enough to say that

I've had healthy relationships just because they didn't Ike Turner me.

Unlike Rachel's parents, mine provided me with a surplus of bad examples. Effectually, I've spent my adult life seeking out good ones. For instance, do not get involved with a fifty-year-old, chronically depressed, unemployed alcoholic who still gets high and is trying to make it as a musician. Thanks, Mom.

Healthy wasn't something I had dedicated much thought to, and therein lay the problem. The mere idea of it made me sweat. Quick, think. Think, damn it! When that failed, I tried to evoke the power of Taoism's Wu Wei, which instructs you to not think about something, in hope that the answer will magically appear. No luck there either. I knew the answer had to be something simple, but what? Though if people like Rachel, the very fruit of healthy loins, were having trouble figuring out how to make it happen, what chance did I have? None.

Ten minutes into our first night in Valencia, I fell while attempting to drunkenly hurdle a bush on a dare. The fall badly sprained my ankle, which I proceeded to walk on, pretending like always that I was fine. The last thing I wanted was to admit is that I got injured doing something stupid. I may have been drunk but my pride was fully sober. Consequently, I walked around town for two hours before my ankle swelled to the size of a grapefruit, at which point my injury could no longer be denied.

"Ready to leave?" I asked Rachel. She was my best friend in Santiago. Though we had only known each other for six months, we would often joke that we were like a cute old married couple. Both of us were on our own in a foreign country, so we depended on each other in a way you don't normally do with people you've just met. We did everything together. Hence, when she told me she wanted to stay in order to spend some more time with Evan, a guy she had just met, I felt a little hurt. Telling her this, however, wasn't an option.

As a child, I was taught emotions were not things you express but weapons you carry. Watching my mother's emotional outbursts terrified me. I dealt with Mom's fits like one would react to meeting a bear in the forest, by remaining silent and motionless, but most importantly, by always avoiding eye contact. To do so would be considered a provocation. On the bright side, I became really good at playing dead. Not surprisingly, I grew to fear my own emotions, associating them with traumatizing experiences.

My other option was to adopt my father's philosophy when it comes to problems, to let it be. Strangely, I don't think this is what Lennon meant. Part of me knew that ignoring my feelings wasn't the best way to deal with a problem, but if only given a choice between berating people and stifling my emotions, I choose stifling.

While I've come to realize that none of my reactions are a healthy way to handle a problem, undoing a quarter century of bad habits is like debunking an accepted truth. For when you reach a certain age, after learning the truth about Santa, the Tooth Fairy, and pro wrestling, you tend to think there's little life can throw your way that will surprise you. Despite being an adult, I too live in this fragile bubble comprised of ultimate truths. Like a child, my heart breaks with every illusion shattered. Pluto is not a planet. A tomato is not a vegetable. Sometimes people let you down.

"We can go with you," Karin offered, pointing to Sarah and herself. Karin and Sarah were classmates of Rachel's. Tall, young, and attractive, Karin was the wholesome daughter of two ministers in Maine. As for Sarah, she was your typical Midwesterner, blonde, and built like someone raised on meat and potatoes. I had met them once or twice before the trip, and though we were all friendly, I wouldn't have called them friends. Still, I wasn't in a position to refuse help, so I said, "Great!"

Early the next morning, I woke up to discover my foot was worse. "You should go to the doctor," Rachel muttered in a half sleep, having arrived home only four hours earlier.

"I'm fine," I replied, the way a girl does when she's not really fine. To be sure, I was still upset with Rachel, but more than that, I hate going to hospitals. Going to the doctor requires admitting I'm not well. Even if I know this to be true, it's still not something I like to accept, much less show others. However, Rachel was right. I needed to go. Did I think I could hop on one foot the entire weekend around Santiago and then to the airport? Yes, I did.

Rachel came with me to the emergency room and patiently sat by my side as the doctors looked at my chameleon foot, whose colors and size changed by the minute. The sight of it in broad daylight and while sober made me break into tears. "I'm so ugly," I sobbed, vanity always being my first priority. Several hours later, my ankle was bandaged up and I was released. "Don't expect to walk for about three weeks," the doctor said.

Missing Las Fallas was out of the question. I had been looking forward to it all year. Every spring, artists will erect giant papier-maché figures with the objective of making their displays as outlandish as possible. The year I went, there was an evil Geppetto standing above a confused Pinocchio. While the displays are quite impressive on their own, the word fallas in Spanish means torch. Since a festival is not a festival in Spain without fire, the culminating night is celebrated by lighting the floats, which are filled with firecrackers, on fire. However, what makes this spectacle even more alluring to Americans like me, is that from a Western standpoint, there are little to no safety precautions taken, as drunken people and even small children are free to dance around the fires. This was going to be a once in a lifetime opportunity.

The apartment we rented for the weekend was on the outskirts of town, far from the festival's main events. That night, I took a cab to the city center and attempted to make my way through Valencia's crowded streets, which of course were cobblestoned. Every step was like an obstacle course. Further compounding my problems, my crutches were not your usual American kind that rest in your armpit, but hand crutches, which force you to place all your weight into the palm of your hand. Jesus Christ, did it hurt. He at least had a reason to endure the pain; I however, was not saving humanity, but instead being punished for drunken stupidity.

As much as I didn't want to admit it, I needed help getting around and more than anyone, I wanted that help from my best friend. Yet every time I looked for Rachel, she was running off with Evan.

"Wait, how are you two related again?" Karin had asked me earlier that day, referring to Evan.

"My deaf gay brother and his gay brother got married last summer and just adopted three deaf Mexican-American kids. So I guess we're like family, but through marriage."

"Oh, but have you guys ever...?"

"No. Kinda. I mean, not really. We've always been flirty, but it's more of a running joke in our family. I guess, even though we're not blood-related it still feels... taboo."

Fortunately, Karin and Sarah didn't mind walking slowly with me as I crutched along, one block every ten minutes.

Though when we finally arrived to the center of town, it was clear that it was no place for a cripple.

The festivities kicked off at midnight and at a quarter to, people began to swarm the streets. Within minutes we were gridlocked. Trying to get a better view, streams of people came shoving through and that's when I heard it. Like a broken record, it just kept repeating in my head: help, I've fallen and I can't get up.

Oh my god, I thought, this is how I die. Somebody is going to push me down and I'm going to get trampled like Mufasa in The Lion King. I looked for Rachel but she wasn't there.

Realizing I was completely helpless, I began to bawl hysterically and so did my roommate Kathrin. Frantic, I tried to find a way out and saw Evan about to get into a fight. Then, just when I thought all was lost, Karin grabbed me and braced me against the crowd until we could escape into the Burger King behind us.

Thinking our nightmare was over, Rachel dug through her purse and asked, "Where's my wallet?" Karin's was missing as well. Defeated, we started to make our way back to the apartment without having seen a single fire.

After the fires were extinguished, hundreds of thousands of people took to the streets. There wasn't a taxi in sight. Lines for buses went on for blocks and would probably take hours. While the rest of the group could easily walk the three kilometers back to the apartment, me with my crutches wouldn't make it.

My hands were already blistered from having crutched around for three hours. As it was, I had no strength left to make it back on crutches.

Rallying together, one by one everyone took turns carrying me. At first, they gave me piggyback rides. Unfortunately, this didn't last very long. My arms, weakened from having to support myself on hand crutches all night, gave out. That's when the carrying got really interesting.

First, they attempted to carry me the way you see people lugging dead bodies on TV. Sarah got my arms and Karin my feet. When that failed, they tried putting me on Evan's shoulders, like a small child at a parade. I was too weak to sit up, so Karin and Sarah held my arms out for support, forming a sort of retarded cheerleader pose. Even Aaron with his bum knee pitched in and tried to carry me. All the while, random people cheered us on, thinking we were drunk or participating in some sort of competition.

Despite everyone's collective effort, an hour later, we were still a kilometer from the apartment. Luckily, a cab drove by soon enough. Sarah and Karin managed to flag it down, and rode back with me. Our trip to Valencia may have been a disaster, but it solidified our friendships.

Later that night, as I laid in bed – which I shared with Rachel and Evan due to a lack of adequate accommodation – I turned to Rachel and said, "You know, I needed you this weekend and you weren't there." As I said it, I could feel the corners of my mouth start to curl, forming a smile. It felt so good to finally be honest. Meanwhile, Rachel began to cry as she apologized profusely declaring herself the worst friend in the world. It didn't feel fair that while she bawled miserably, I felt oddly fulfilled. Yet for the first time, I meant it when I said, "It's fine."

como se dice

Learning a different language as an adult is downright demeaning. For one, programs talk to you as if you were a child. Repeat: *The dog is brown. It is sunny.* Better programs teach you more useful phrases, such as: *I lived in New York for seven years... Viví en Nueva York durante siete años.* Yet even these exhaust themselves two minutes into a conversation, and rightly so, any longer would make you look like some kind of weather fanatic or freak. More importantly, talking about the weather doesn't help you make friends. This is something I learned the hard way, after moving to Spain. No one wants to be friends with the weird weather kid, nor do you want to be known as the weather kid.

Trying to control the conversation by asking questions is also futile. I hoped it would allow me to practice my Spanish in a controlled way, figuring I could look up the questions in advance and then rattle them off the next time I was at a party, impressing people with my superb Spanish skills. However, this idea quickly fell by the wayside. Eventually the conversation veers into an unpredicted subject, or the person gives a much too elevated response for my five-year-old vocabulary, and I'm left trying to force the conversation back to its original course. Then in a panic, I'll revert back to canned questions learned from various programs. How old are you? How many siblings do you have? What are their names? What's your favorite food? What do you do on the weekends? At what time do you "stand up" in the morning? The questions are very specific and if you're not careful, it's easy to come across as a stalker. Nothing about this is organic.

Like many other Americans, my experience with foreign language comes primarily from public schooling. Three years in high school along with one year in college of Spanish, and all I can remember is como se dice... which translates to, how do you say... Crucial, if you ask me.

The sad thing is I passed all my tests, papers, and classes. According to my resume, I'm conversational! Don't act like you haven't lied a little on your resume. Frankly, I never figured it would matter. When am I ever going to need to know the word for dandruff in Spanish? Now that I'm living in Spain, I've realized, I DO NEED TO KNOW THIS WORD! If only I could go back in time and talk some sense into my twenty-year-old self. Pay attention! Do not drop out of Spanish to take Gaelic! It's not worth having less class time!

My inability to speak another language never bothered me until the summer after Gums and I broke up, and I traveled to France with Soraya. There, I managed to pick up a French lover, Jean Michel. Unlike other French men, who try to kiss you the minute you're within arm's reach, he was quiet and reserved. Like a romance movie from the forties, we met by chance on the streets of Nice. Naturally, it was my last night in town.

It was two a.m. and all of the bars in Nice were closing. As a way to kill time before our six a.m. flight, my girlfriends and I began to wander the streets. Not long after, we ran into Jean Mi and his group of friends, out celebrating his twenty-eighth birthday. It didn't take much convincing for them to leap at the opportunity to entertain three pretty girls for a few hours.

I was standing to the side, my arms folded, ready to fend off men, when Jean Mi came up to me. With his head tucked down, shrugging his shoulders, he quickly said, "Hello!" before quietly ducking behind his friends. I found his shyness endearing. "He doesn't speak much English," his friend explained. As for me, the only words I knew in French were please, thank you, and I love you, none of which applied to my present situation. Alas, Jean Mi was not about to let this insignificant detail stand in the way of romancing a pretty foreign girl.

"American?" he asked. I nodded and he immediately proceeded to rattle off every American show he knew. Sex and the City! Simpsons! Family Guy! Nip-Tuck! One of the things

I've learned through traveling is that American pop culture is a universal language.

After he exhausted his list, he pulled out his phone and began showing me all of his American music. Wu-Tang Clan, Beyoncé, Ricky Martin. Upon hearing the last one, I shot him a sideways glance. Picking up on my signal, he jumped to his defense, "No, I like girl!" I laughed, thinking, really? Ricky Martin is what made him feel a need to reassert his sexuality? Not his fanny purse? But Europe's funny like that. Even so, it was interesting to see that Ricky Martin translates in French the same as it does in English: gay.

A few European cites later, I returned to the U.S. and began my last year of teaching in Brooklyn. My European adventure had filled me with delicious cured meat, cheese, and a newfound resolve to move abroad.

Through the help of Google Translate, Jean Mi and I began exchanging e-mails and thus began our courting. He wrote me every day, several times a day. While very sweet, his messages were also terribly translated. I tried my best to piece his actual messages together though mostly without success.

Exhibit A:

I found some pictures on the web like that you can walk a bit you with us, you'll have more than to imagine that you're behind the bike, I would not drive too fast but he'll have to hold on to me! If one day you come back to Nice, I would bring you the best route to

a motorcycle, I myself was impressed by the beauty of the landscape.
I hope this wish will be fulfilled as well, and I gave you want to
come back!

One could only imagine how my e-mails translated. One
time I thought I had finished an e-mail with kisses kisses.
However, when Jean Mi emailed me back he gave me an
impromptu French lesson featuring the different usages of
embrasser, which also happens to mean fuck. Have a good
day! Fuck fuck, Ali. This is why American girls are considered
sluts abroad.

We e-mailed back and forth for weeks before we worked up
the courage to take our relationship to the next level, Skype.
The first time we talked over Skype, we were so nervous
that we both bought bottles of wine. Every time we couldn't
understand each other, which turned out to be often, we'd
toast, "Santé!" then drink. Like most awkward situations that
involve sexual tension, the alcohol proved to be an effective
social lubricator. Once we got the hang of it, Skype became
our addiction.

We would talk on Skype every day, for hours. Though we
didn't share a common language, with the help of Google
Translate we had amazing conversations. At first, it was easy
to open up. With so much distance between us it didn't matter
what we said. Our two worlds had no way of colliding. So I
told him about my mom and he told me about his. I even told

him about Gums. I remember he asked me, "Why are you single?"

"Because my heart's broken," I said.

"Mine too," he replied.

Through Skype, we'd chat about our dreams, our fears, and sometimes we'd simply sit and look at one another, smiling. We even Skyped while we slept. With the six-hour time difference, I'd watch him sleep as I cooked dinner. Likewise, he would watch me sleep as he ate breakfast. I'd wake up only to see him watching The Simpsons dubbed in French and eating a midday snack. He'd smile, acknowledging me, then carry on like I was right there in the room, a normal part of his daily routine. In time, and over Skype, we fell in a lot of like.

I promised to return and learn French. He promised to learn English and cook me French food. For two months I studied French before returning to France. Sadly, my French had not much improved, as when I arrived all I could say was, il fait beau. The weather is nice. This was the first thing I said to him at the airport when I went to visit him that November over Thanksgiving weekend, as we pulled away from our initial embrace. Romantic, right?

Of course, I learned other words during my studies, such as red car. But as you can imagine, pointing to objects randomly, then naming them and their color, isn't very attractive. I felt bad. Here he was expecting a romantic weekend and instead he's stuck babysitting a small child just learning to talk.

Like a child, I only knew how to express my essential needs, such as hunger. "J'ai fame," I'd say. A phrase I came to use often during our weekend together as I am always hungry. Luckily, my friends who speak French taught me a few more important phrases—take off your clothes is deshabille-toi. Sadly, this was not utilized much during our weekend together.

My fears were confirmed: without Google Translate, we had nothing. The passion that so clearly resonated across Skype was absent as we sat face to face. Without language it was hard to feel intimate, have silly times, or create those inside jokes that come with being a couple. My last night in town he took me out to dinner and at last, parts of his personality started to peek through. I got a sense of his silly side. We laughed and a part of me also wanted to cry. Too little too late. I'm leaving tomorrow, I thought.

After that weekend, our romance ended and I returned to Brooklyn. We continued to talk weekly; however, our relationship eventually dwindled to that of pen pals. Though to be fair, it would have never worked. I'm a twice-a-day kind of girl and he's a twice-a-week kind of guy.

To be sure, Jean Mi was not my last foreign fling. A year later I moved to Spain and the very first person I met was a beautiful hostel worker who went by the name Nacho, which is short for Ignacio. Tall, dark, and handsome, he was the epitome of what every girl dreams of meeting once stepping off a plane in a foreign country. Plus, unlike Jean Mi, Nacho spoke English well. After checking me in and carrying my suitcase up, he directed me to what I still consider one of the best restaurants in town. It was definite brownie points for him.

During my two-week stay at the hostel I saw quite a lot of Nacho. Though I desperately wanted to flirt with him, part of me wondered if that wouldn't be crossing the line that so sacredly divides hostel workers and their guests. There was no way to be sure our interactions were the result of sexual tension and not just a simple display of hospitality. It's his job to be nice, I told myself. Besides, he's a man, and men like him are only after one thing, a good rating on Hostelworld. Unsure how to conduct myself around him, I acted like a twitterpated teenage girl and bombarded him a million asinine questions just to get his attention: "Where's the best place to buy cheap groceries? Good shoes? What time do people generally go out?"

So it continued, until one day when I asked him, "Can I book another night with you?"

"Another night with me, at my apartment?" he jested. The comment made me blush. Hearing his wit only made me like him more. Trying to run with it, I quipped back,

"Oh! I hadn't realized that was an option!" Right when I said it, the mood quickly shifted. He regained composure and booked another night for me at the hostel. Had I taken it a step too far? Perhaps we hadn't been flirting at all. Crushed, I accepted our banter for what it was, an ESL misunderstanding of the meaning, with you.

A few days later, while asking him yet another question, he surprised me and asked me one in return, "What are you doing for lunch?"

"Huh?" I eloquently replied.

"Are you coming back here to the hostel?"

"Yes, probably," I stammered, wondering why he would ask.

"I'm going to make some fish. Would you like to have lunch with me?" Without hesitation, I answered, sure. But what I really wanted to say was, "I love you too."

When I returned to the hostel at lunch, I found Nacho already hard at work on our four-course meal. "Can I help you with anything?" I offered. "No," he said, shooting a huge smile at me. As he cooked, we talked. We talked for six hours, smoking and drinking wine. Just as I did with Jean Mi, Nacho and I shared our passions, our dreams, even our childhoods. It wasn't like any other conversations I'd had before with hostel workers, which consisted of directions or logistical information. Our conversation was something commonly found amongst new friends or perhaps, new lovers.

The day I checked out, I gave Nacho my number. "Thanks for everything," I said, handing him a torn piece of paper.

"What's this?" he asked.

"My number," I said, although it came out more like a question. His reaction mortified me.

"Yes, well, I'm sure we'll run into each other in the city," he replied. "There are only a few places to go, but I will use it nevertheless."

I left knowing he wouldn't. I was right. I'm still waiting for his call. After I moved into my apartment, I'd periodically check the news, searching for headlines like Happy Hostel Worker Viciously Eaten by Rabid Bear. It's not that I wished him harm; I just wanted an answer, a reason for why he never called.

Eventually I discovered through a friend that Nacho had a girlfriend. "But he cooked for me!" I whined. "He cooked for me twice!" How had I been so wrong in interpreting the situation? Different countries have different customs, but I figured the laws of attraction were universal. Weren't they? Obsessed with getting answers, I asked every Spanish guy I met, "If you cook for a girl, does that mean you like her?"

"No! Does that mean something in the U.S?"

"Yes! In the U.S., a guy only cooks for you if he likes you. Wouldn't your girlfriend be angry if you cooked for another girl?"

"No, everyone has to eat." When Rachel's roommate told me this, I paused, thinking, if dinner is casual, then what's considered a move?

Six months later I ran into Nacho on the street. After waiting months and months to see him again, this was not at all how I envisioned our reunion going—me with a sprained ankle and crutches, trying to hop to the grocery store as I huddled underneath a broken umbrella. I tried to imagine a worse scenario, but none came to mind.

Bracing myself, I waited for Nacho to come up and say something to me, but he just averted his eyes and walked right by. With my mouth agape, I watched as he tried to enter the store in front of me, actively ignoring me. Had I been a person quickly walking by with their headphones, a random face in the crowd, then that would be one thing. However, with my crutches and umbrella, I was something of a spectacle. Ignoring me would have been as easy as ignoring a legless dog. I'm sure it took a large amount of restraint on his part. Were it not for my ankle, I would have run away, angrily muttering to myself. Regrettably, all I could do was slowly hobble away, further prolonging this painful reunion. Now I could vividly imagine a worse scenario.

Had I known this is how it would play out, I wouldn't have spent all that time idealizing this moment, wondering if what we had was really chemistry or a strange cultural misunderstanding. I'm surprised we hadn't run into each other sooner. Like he said, Santiago's a small town. With a hurt ankle and pride, I hobbled home with the help of Rachel. Then, turning to her, I asked, "Como se dice asshole en español?"

the breakup

In the spring of 2010, a friend's dad was diagnosed with lung cancer. He had smoked for almost thirty years before finally deciding to quit. Six months later, as a parting gift from his longtime companion, cigarettes, he received a tumor the size of a grapefruit attached to his heart and lungs. It was in the late stages and statistically speaking, he didn't have much time.

Everyone knows smoking is a dangerous habit; it says so right on the carton, though this never seems to stop anyone. Like many, I've witnessed smoking claim the lives of loved ones. My father's mother, Grandma Shirley, smoked until the day she died from issues caused by smoking. I can still picture her, sitting in my living room, hooked up to an oxygen tank. The sight terrified me, so I pretended she was an astronaut, and that her heavy inhales and exhales were due to atmospheric changes on the moon.

As for my father, he smoked until he had a serious heart attack at the ripe old age of forty-nine. In the hospital, the doctor gave him an ultimatum: quit smoking or die. Years later I asked him if it was difficult to quit like that, cold turkey. He said it was the easiest decision he ever made. "It was a wake-up call. You don't get any more after that." He had a point.

Since she was sixteen, my mother has smoked Marlboros. Similar to cereal boxes, Marlboro used to offer rewards for mail in carton tops. Prizes varied, but one option was a travel bag worth something like 1,000 points. Growing up, my mother smoked so much that she earned not one, but four huge red bags with Marlboro written in giant letters across the sides. Every time I flew cross-country to see my dad and brothers I used the Marlboro bag. Back then, I was too young to realize that I was a walking advertisement for Marlboro, recruiting other young children to smoke as I cheerily stood there, bag in hand, waiting for my father to pick me up. Above me there should have been a sign that read, I'm a straight-A student, and my cigarette of choice is Marlboro. The thought still makes me shudder. Consider this my PSA.

Even though I didn't have the best relationship with my mother, I surely didn't want her to die a slow painful death. My friend's news fresh in my mind, I picked up the phone and called.

"How are you?" I asked.

"Ugh, my throat's acting up again," she rasped and I pictured that scary anti-smoking commercial from the nineties in which the woman takes a puff of her cigarette from a hole in her throat. Scary, but effective.

Though I already knew the answer, I asked, "What's a-matter with your throat?"

"It's infected, and my thyroids are the size of kiwis," she said. Sounds like an exaggeration, but I'm sure she was telling the truth. The last time it happened we were at dinner. I looked up from my menu and saw that my mother had suddenly turned into a human blowfish. Like the hole-in-the-throat commercial, the vision haunted me, which was exactly the reason why I had called. I was worried. Thus, despite my better judgment, I told her, "Well, the smoking probably doesn't help. What happened to quitting?" E-4, hit.

Though we weren't playing Battleship, my mother interpreted my question as an attack. "How dare you tell me how to live my life," she hissed, adding, "I don't say anything about the way you live yours!"

"What?"

"How I'm uncomfortable with your drinking habits or your relationship with God," she continued.

At hearing this, my eyes bulged out like a Looney Tunes character. Drinking habits? Had she forgotten my secret superhero identity? The one-drink wonder? The mere smell of liquor is enough to get me buzzed because I hardly ever drink. As for the God comment, I can only imagine it's because I refuse to attend her "church" which, with its rock bands and jumbo prayer screen, is more like a show in Vegas than a place of worship. The church may not have had tigers, but it did have cougars, e.g., my mom.

After letting out a heavy sigh, she finally answered my question. "No. Okay. I've got a lot going on right now, all right? Excuse me if I don't up and quit because you tell me to. It's my life. I can do what I want with it."

"I'm worried about you. You're my mom. Your health affects me." In remaining calm, I hoped we could have a constructive conversation. However, trying to take the high road never fails to piss off my mom, who interprets my maturity as evidence of a superiority complex.

"You think you're so goddamn perfect, don't you!" she sneered.

I was tempted to say, "Well, you don't set the bar too high." She was right. I did think I was better. For one, I wasn't a fifty-four-year-old woman dating a twenty-six-year-old who still lived at home. Nor was I throwing a tantrum. She made it so easy. Nevertheless, I bit my tongue.

Not that it mattered. The conversation didn't get much further before I got fed up and had to hang up.

She stopped calling after that.

My mom's smoking has always been a touchy subject. When her best friend of twenty years suggested that she might want to quit, my mom stopped speaking to her. Ask her what happened and she'll tell you, "She thinks she can tell me how

to live my life. Well, I won't be pushed around any longer!"
They didn't speak for years. The same was true when my aunt
brought up my mom's little "habit."

Excommunication is common on my mom's side of the
family. In some respects, it's like your average flu, annoying
to be sure, but hardly cause for alarm since everyone knows
it'll pass, only to come back again next season. Unfortunately,
there is no shot to help you prevent excommunication in my
family. Consequently, everyone is subject to its random will.

This was the first time I had stopped talking to my mom.
Weeks had passed without a single call. While tempted to let
the feud go on a little longer, her birthday rolled around and
begrudgingly, I called. It was one of those times you pray for
voicemail. Luckily, the next best thing happened: my sister
answered my mom's cell. Thus began our game of telephone.

"Hey, where's Mom?" I asked.

"Doing her makeup," Monika said.

"Oh. Um, tell her I say Happy Birthday."

"She says 'thanks.'"

"Ask her what she's doing for her birthday."

"Says she's going to dinner."

"That's nice...well, tell her to have a great day."

Realizing we had hit a new low, I hung up and looked up
therapists in my area.

● ● ● ● ●

Later that week, at dinner, I told the story to my friend Ann, who said, "Al, you wouldn't let your boyfriend or friends treat you like this, would you?"

I told her no and she said, "So then why would you allow your mother, the person who's supposed to love and support you, treat you this way?" Ann was a hairdresser, so she's very good at sorting out people's problems.

"She's not just anyone," I said. "She's my mother."

"Exactly! She's your mother, the last person who is supposed to treat you like this."

Once again, she made a good point. Still, I wasn't ready to give up on my mom. "That's why I start therapy tomorrow," I said, raising my glass for a toast. "To being an official New Yorker!"

Therapy was a last resort. I had seen therapists before, unsuccessfully. After Monika's visit to the hospital, my mom insisted we all go to family therapy. Though it started well enough, fifteen minutes into the session my mom turned to me and revealed the true root of our problems. "You didn't send me a birthday card!" she complained. Then she really got going, "You never ask me how my day is! You don't take an interest in my life or friends."

Rather than refute her arguments, I listened. Her and my issues were just that, hers and mine—no one else's. Still, I give my mom credit; she was attempting to fix our problem. That was the most proactive I would ever see her.

Sadly, my second attempt at therapy proved as lame as the first. Perhaps the problem was that I expected my therapist to be my fairy godfather. When we started, I waited for my therapist to wave his magic wand and bestow upon me an answer, a cure, medication, something; yet he did nothing of the sort.

Looking back, I'm not sure if I really understood how therapy worked. After laying all of my problems on the table within the first two sessions, I came into the third not knowing what to talk about. After about two minutes of small talk, we fell into silence. Unlike in those times where silence is comforting, my therapist's silence was as awkward as a bad first date. Always a people pleaser, I found myself talking and telling stories just to entertain him. When my party anecdotes exhausted themselves, I began looking up topical references, plane crashes, book reviews, reality TV. Though we did talk sporadically about my problems with my mother, each time just felt pointless, like chewing baby food.

Three months into therapy, I was still the same person with the same problems. If anything, therapy made me more frustrated. I eventually did have my "aha" moment. Though not with help from my fairy godfather, but rather from my co-teacher.

"I feel terrible," Lydia told me. "Last night I was so tired, I snapped at Stephanie. Anyway, I talked to Stephanie afterwards and apologized and I think she understands."

Dumbfounded, I asked, "You apologized to an eight-year-old?"

"Well, yeah," Lydia replied.

A few days later I told the story to my therapist, who asked, "So you're looking for an apology from your mom?"

"No, I want acknowledgement, that she messed up, that things weren't perfect. She needs to accept some responsibility."

"So you want an apology," he repeated.

"No," I said. "I want to forgive her."

"How can you forgive someone who doesn't apologize?" he asked. "You can't."

"So what do I do?" I asked.

He shrugged his shoulders and sat there smiling at me, waiting for me to say something as always.

When it comes to breakups, there are some you plan, and there are some that just happen naturally. However, breaking up with your mom is not something you plan or expect to happen naturally. Instead, like two mature adults, my mom and I broke up through Facebook. Right before I moved to Spain, she posted on my wall: It would be nice if you remembered you had a mother, a brother, and a sister. In general, my mom and I spoke about once a week, Saturday mornings, around

noon my time. Last time we spoke it was Sunday, so it being
Wednesday, not three days later, her comment confused me.

Maybe I'd feel more impetus to call her if we had a better
relationship or more in common. I'd pass something while
walking, be reminded of her, and call. Every girl longs to
have a relationship like the Gilmore Girls, where mother and
daughter share inside jokes and talk about everything, at warp
speed, for hours on end. However, my mother and I were the
antithesis of Rory and Lorelei.

Despite coming from her womb and sharing her DNA,
I was nothing like my mother, and quite frankly, I preferred
it that way. It made it easier for me to distinguish her from
me, crazy from the sane, a way to tell myself, I am not like
you. Whether I have made it a point to assert my differences
from my mother, or if we actually are different, is debatable.
There are times when I myself question if I have come to hate
something solely because my mom likes it, or vice versa, love
it because she hates it. Though there are some things that I
can say with complete certainty I do not like. For instance, hot
pink Uggs, or Fuggs as I call them. Not a fan, never was, never
will be. Meanwhile, that says my mom is all over it.

Over the years my relationship with my mother deteriorated
to that of a miserable married couple, staying together for the
sake of the kids. Our communication was mostly superficial,
meant to mask all the things that went unsaid. Consequently,
come each weekend we'd have nothing to say to one another.

Toward the end, the tension grew so strong that it no longer felt like an elephant, but a whale in the room. Every time she called, that's all I could imagine, a beached whale slowly dying in the corner.

As a result, I'd limit our conversations to ten minutes max. Mass transit became my main scapegoat. "Op! Going into a tunnel," or "Hopping on the subway, gotta go!" Had her Facebook comment been a phone conversation, I would have probably done the same and avoided the issue by blaming it on a crowded bar, taxis, whatever it took. However, there is no subway equivalent when it comes to the Internet. Just as well, the whale could not be ignored any longer.

That's funny, I don't remember my phone ringing, I wrote as a comment. It was my hint to her; if you have something to say, call me. If she wanted to play passive-aggressive then we'd play passive-aggressive.

True to form, she retorted with a much longer, angrier, and even less discrete post on my Facebook wall, a completely appropriate place to have a family discussion. Immediately after, she updated her status to Tired of being nice to people who are mean. Is it weird that I wanted to press the Like button on that one? It made me laugh! Online name-calling! Come on, what are we? Bloggers?

Her post reminded me of when I was thirteen and having my first fight with Soraya. We were at a friend's house and furious with one another for a reason I can no longer remember, so it was clearly important. Instead of talking about it we stood by the radio, glaring at each other as we fought over which "I hate you" song to play. I'd put on Stay Away by Nirvana, and after a few chords she'd press stop then switch to How You Remind Me by Nickelback. Three songs later, we were hugging each other, crying and apologizing profusely. We didn't know any better.

Eleven years later I found myself having the same fight with my mother, only I wasn't thirteen and neither was she. But that's exactly what my mom's post was: a teenage girl's sad attempt to say "I'm upset" to someone she loves, because she doesn't know how to use her words.

Following the Facebook incident, I sent my mom an e-mail. I think we both want a healthy relationship, mom. We just need to work on it. I can't be happy if we continue to have this relationship, so either work on this with me, or don't be a part of my life because I'm ready to move on.

It was an ultimatum.

Knowing my mother well, I had a hunch what she would say, not that it mattered. Just as in my past failed relationships, I knew that the ultimatum wasn't for her; it was for me. I needed to feel like I had said and done everything in my power to fix things. So when she replied, You have a mother, a wonderful, insightful, caring mother!!!! I have given you all that I could. I won't try to convince you otherwise, I wasn't so much hurt as I was disappointed, a part of me hoping she'd prove me wrong. Maybe she didn't see it, but we had a choice.

synecdoche

Unlike some girls, who grow up planning their perfect wedding, I grew up dreaming of the perfect elopement. Like I told my friend Rachel, I want to wake up one day next to the man I want to marry and have him ask, "How would you feel about getting married today?" Then we'd run away together and write a happier ending to *The Graduate*. It's not that I'm afraid of commitment, but rather of all the stress that comes with getting married. Of course, this doesn't pertain to all weddings in general, just the ones where my family is involved.

This is particularly true when it comes to my mom's side of the family, which is Filipino, and as a result, full of alpha females. Unlike other Asian cultures, Filipino women are considered the head of the household. Having grown up somewhat removed from Filipino culture, I thought it rather strange that my uncle drove my aunt around everywhere as if he were her personal chauffeur. "Doesn't your mom have a driver's license?" I asked my cousin.

"Yeah, but that's what all the Filipino husbands do," she explained. "They drive their wives to parties and drop them off."

"So that they don't drive drunk?" I asked.

"No, just 'cause."

Taking this new information into account when playing bride, I would recite my new pretend vows so that they included "to drive, in sickness and in health." While I've since learned that this peculiarity only applies to the women of my mother's generation, as a frequent passenger, a part of me still wishes this was actually part of the bargain when agreeing to marry.

With a family full of outspoken females, it's really no surprise that whenever we get together there's always some sort of power struggle. I imagine it's what a World Summit meeting would look like if there weren't set protocols, agendas, and security. Somebody please tell China to stop telling Tibet to get that mole checked, we already discussed that last month. She's seeing somebody about it.

Understandably, I knew that my cousin's wedding would be no different.

The day of the dress rehearsal, we were all sitting around my aunt's living room playing Scattergories when my little brother Kyle, attempting to name a medicine that starts with the letter S, said "Sin-ak-doe-ché."

"Bullshit!" I exclaimed. "You made that up."

Offended, he employed the classic defense, "No, I didn't!"
"So then what does it do?" I asked.

"It regulates blood pressure," my cousin's fiancé, a pharmacist, chimed in. "Yeah, it's real popular in Canada," he assured me, winking at Kyle.

Though neither one of us were winning, what bothered me was the principle. I was right! Admittedly, it's a fault of mine. Over the years, my need to be right has become pathological, to the point where I'll find myself arguing things I know to be false just to avoid conceding. It just so happened that in this particular instance, I knew I was right. There was no such medication or word for that matter. I may have had no way of proving it, but I knew they were lying.

Not long after, my mom walked in. Having heard us from the other room, she said jokingly, "Why don't we all cool down?" She had a water bottle in her hand and, reading the mischievous look on her face, I got up and began backing away. I knew exactly what she was about to do.

Back when I still lived in California, my mom and I had a habit of chasing each other around the house, throwing food or water at one another. If those options weren't available, we'd resort to giving one another wet willies, snapping each other's bras, or towel-whipping one another. Sometimes, Monika and Kyle would get involved and in which case, we'd gang up on Kyle and give him wedgies. Usually, it was all in good fun.

Then again, usually, we were in the comfort in our own home. This was different.

Not in the mood to play our customary game of cat and mouse, I walked away, waving my hands above my head to signal surrender. When this didn't work, I attempted a verbal surrender, "I'm not playing anymore. Mom, stop." And then she did, seconds later, after successfully drenching me, and my only change of clothes, in water.

Five minutes later, we were fighting, but not because she had thrown water on me. Rather, the fight arose because after she was done messing around, she expected me to clean up her mess, which is more or less the same fight we've been having for over a decade. "Here," she said, tossing me a roll of paper towel, "clean it up."

"Excuse me?" I scoffed. "You poured it. You pick it up. I told you to stop." This, to my mother, was like a slap in the face. For in Filipino culture, children are taught to respect their elders, regardless of whether they are right or wrong.

"It's like the story of Chicken Little," an aunt told me. "Don't be like Chicken Little."

"What? I don't think that's what the story's saying…" I tried to tell her, but she told me I shouldn't talk back.

By refusing to clean up, I was talking back and embarrassing my mother, in front of our whole family. In an effort to avoid making a scene, I asked my cousin for a change of clothes and walked away.

synecdoche

The morning after the wedding, my entire family and I went out to a brunch buffet, or fine dining, as they call it in Jersey. Well into my third helping, my brother whispered from across the table, "Sin ak doc-ché—" as if to taunt me.

"Is not a word!" I replied indignantly.

"Yes it is! I learned it in English," he said in his usual cheery voice.

Smiling, I retorted, and rather snootily, "Well, I took AP English and I'll bet you anything there's no such word."

"Yes there is!" he insisted, pulling out his smartphone.

Leaning over, I read, "Synecdoche?" then scoffed, "Synecdoche is a word, I'll give you that. But it's not pronounced Sin-ak-doe-ché, like you said it, like it's some type of Mexican food. Plus, it's not a medicine, which means I was right! Ugh. I knew it. Cheater!"

"Whatever," he huffed, excusing himself from the table to get dessert. Content to have been right yet again, I continued shoveling food into my mouth and didn't give the subject much more thought. I was having a Belgian waffle.

Although Kyle had dropped the issue, my mother did not. After brunch she told me, "Go apologize to your brother."

As the youngest and the only boy, Kyle has always been a clear favorite. She is fiercely protective of him and through the years I've watched her treat him like a surrogate boyfriend, a role to which he acquiesced. That's Kyle for you, always a people pleaser. Having been raised by three strong women, can you really blame him?

Still, he's always been somewhat of a mama's boy. Breast-fed until the age of three, I'm not entirely convinced my mother ever detached from Kyle. Before going away to college, she would "joke" about how she intended to follow him. We were all surprised, and relieved, when she didn't.

Thus when she said, "You hurt his feelings. You need to be more sensitive," I brushed her off, thinking she was being overprotective.

"It's not a big deal," I told her. Everyone knows teenagers are moody and sensitive. Besides, it was just a small disagreement, hardly worthy of being dragged out in the middle of a strip-mall parking lot. He'd get over it because that's what siblings do, fight and make up.

To be fair, the three of us didn't fight much growing up. Instead, we spent our childhood devising new ways to playfully torture one another. I'll admit, sometimes we got carried away, like the summer Kyle and I shared a room together. It started on account of Kyle's hygiene.

I was nineteen and back in Sacramento for summer break. Kyle was twelve, and clearly not thrilled at the prospect of sharing his room with his older sister. Neither was I for that matter, for Kyle is what I call a triple threat: a farter, drooler, and snorer. At times it was hard tell if the sounds coming from his side of the room were farts, snores, or a perfect unison of the two. How I didn't die of asphyxiation is still a mystery.

However, far worse, was the Axe body spray he applied to himself every morning to mask the stench he released at night. Although directions on the can suggest a light spray, my brother applied the cologne the way one applies a can of Raid to an invading ant colony, spraying away until there was no life left in the room. This left the room smelling like a European man, reeking of must and cologne. Unable to take it any longer, I hid the can while he was away at basketball practice.

I guess he noticed it was missing because when I returned home later that evening, I found my childhood stuffed animal, Piggy, hanging by a noose in the doorway. "You are a sociopath!" I told him.

In the end, our spats never lasted long. One of us would inevitably make a joke or do something to break the ice. "Hey, Ali, this is what we'd look like if we had no knees," Kyle said, attempting to dismount our bar stool with perfectly straight legs, as he mimicked a life size nutcracker. With newfound appreciation for my knee sockets and my genius baby brother, I kissed his forehead, forgetting he had killed my stuffed animal.

Just as before, I thought our disagreement back in the restaurant was a harmless quip, something that'd blow over. However, judging by his persistence, this was not one of those times. While I didn't want to admit my mother was right, I could feel a distance growing between my siblings and I.

The last time I was back in Sacramento, Monika and I went out to lunch, and in an attempt to fulfill my sisterly duty, I asked how things with her boyfriend were going.

"I think I want to break up with him," she said. When I asked why, she got defensive. "Because he's not Christian," she said, the duh implied.

"But didn't you know that when you guys started dating?" I asked, confused, and this only seemed to frustrate her even more.

"It's just, ugh…. you don't understand," she grumbled and she was right, I didn't. I tried to tell her to explain it to me, but she cut me off with "Forget it."

Not wanting to spoil our lunch before it had started, I quickly changed the subject to body piercings. Monika loved body piercings. That'll be foolproof, I thought. Meanwhile, I made a mental note to avoid all conversations that included boys and God. It felt strange making a list of things I could and could not talk about with my sister, the way you do when you're meeting someone's parents for the first time. Listen, next time you talk to your sister, make sure to avoid mentioning bears, shoehorns, or vegans. Trust me, you'll do great. She'll love you.

After I moved away to New York for college, most of my information on Monika and Kyle came from secondhand

syneodoche

sources. "Did you know that Monika's thinking about moving to L.A.?" my friend Sami told me.

"What?" I said.

"Yeah, she hit Sean up, asking him if he could help her out," he said. Hearing that my ex-boyfriend, who I hadn't talked to in years, knew more about my sister's life than I did felt about as good as using sandpaper as a body loofah.

For a long time, I blamed myself, feeling the distance was a failure on my part. Being the oldest, I was raised to believe it was my responsibility to maintain a good relationship with my younger siblings. Every once in a while, I'd hear the voice of my mother or aunt saying, "You're their ate," which means big sister in Tagalog and moreover, that this was my duty.

Though I try, truthfully, I've never been great at keeping in touch. Now that I live in Spain, it's much easier to use distance as my excuse. Although technology has ruined that too, almost obligating people to stay in constant contact with everyone they've ever known. I'm pretty good at reading e-mails. Replying on the other hand, is an uphill battle. They're just so easy to put off and forget about. I try to Skype, but with the time difference, there's hardly a convenient time to meet. I'll like their posts on Facebook, if that counts for anything.

After the brunch buffet we headed over to Marshalls. I sheepishly followed Kyle, knowing that while I had not been entirely wrong, I wasn't entirely right either. Incapable of finding the words, "I'm sorry," or "I was wrong," I resorted to plan B, bribery. "Need a wallet?" I asked, noticing him eye a black one made of leather. He can't stay mad at me if I buy him something, I thought. Guilt always works.

But he told me, "Naw," with a half smile, which I wanted to think meant, "It's okay." I wanted to ask him if we really were fine, but Marshalls didn't seem like the appropriate place to have a heart to heart, so I dropped it and didn't say anything.

A few months after the wedding, while playing Scrabble, a friend tried to use the word brusque. "That's not a word," I laughed.

"Sure it is," she said, using the word in a sentence.

"Um, I think brisk is the word you're looking for," I replied condescendingly. Intent on settling the matter, Sheela pulled out the dictionary. Clearing her throat, she pointed to a definition, which not only proved that brusque is, in fact, a word but that I am a pompous asshole. Sulking, I awarded Sheela her points.

Though we continued playing, I couldn't help but see it all suddenly spelled out for me, this time in big bold letters. Synecdoche, a literary device employed when a part is used to represent the whole. Kyle had tried to explain it to me at brunch, yet I wouldn't listen. Now, as much as I wanted to brush off my argument with Kyle as I had done hundreds of times before, I knew that the argument, like the word, represented a much bigger, scarier, more complicated truth than I was ready to face.

livestrong

For my mom Julie, who taught me strength.

Like most interesting stories, mine begins before I was even
born, with a woman I never met yet whose story has become
an integral part of my own. Diane was a nice Italian girl, born
and raised in New Jersey and the eldest of Rita and Guy's
four children, first-generation immigrants I would eventually
come to know as Grandma and Grandpa. From what little I've
been told, Diane was a smart, witty, and loving person, hands
down a real catch. Had she not died of breast cancer, I'm sure
she and my dad would still be happily married. Perhaps then,
everything would have been different for my father and two
older brothers. Though "what if" is never a fun game to play.
It's too indulgent, since we'll never have any way of knowing
for sure.

Diane's tale is much too similar to those made-for-TV
movies: woman finds lump, complains to her doctor, gets a bad
diagnosis, three months later it's too late. You sit there in front
of the TV, crying with a box of tissues in your lap, lamenting,

how tragic. It's a story we know all too well, because chances are you have your own Diane. Though I never met Diane, her absence has affected my family and consequently influenced my life. Morbidly, I've always felt somewhat guilty about her death, realizing had she not died I would probably be some other man's daughter, telling a completely different story. But again, enough "what ifs."

It's difficult to imagine how things could have gotten worse for my father, but that's Murphy's Law. During Diane's last few months, my two older brothers, who were three and five at the time, came down with a serious case of meningitis. Thankfully, by some divine intervention or whatever you believe in, they pulled through. Michael made a full recovery. Brian lost his hearing. Diane died. As for my dad, he never did fully recover. He had lost his wife, and a part of him died with Diane.

It's hard to imagine what my dad might have been like before Diane, a man more carefree and open. Part of me wants to picture him as a Bollywood character, prancing in a field and merrily picking flowers to the tune of a sitar, a huge grin slapped across his face. While I can't prove that my father knows bhangra, I know my father was once a sillier man.

One of my favorite stories that my father tells is about the time he and his high school classmates tied a horse to the church bell in the middle of the night. "The horse was so scared it starts shitting everywhere. And the priest hears the bell ringing, right, so he goes up to the church, walks in, and because it's so dark, he goes sliding in the shit. Then comes in another priest, and same thing, down he goes. And me and my buddies are just in the bushes laughing, but really I'm thinking to myself, holy shit." Having told the story countless times, he'll deliver the last line flawlessly, tears streaming down his face from cackling.

My father never told stories like this about Diane. Sure, he'd answer questions, like how they met—bagging groceries at A&P—but his answers never turned into anecdotes. It was as if her cancer had eclipsed all of his happy memories of Diane. Feeling it wasn't my place, I didn't push him to elaborate. Plus, part of me understood my father's reluctance. Casually bringing up someone's cancer into a conversation isn't easy. I've tried.

During my second year of teaching in Brooklyn, my stepmom Julie was diagnosed with breast cancer. Immediately after I found out, I went to call her, but before I could press dial, it occurred to me, what would I say? After spending so many years thinking cancer was a bad word, I suddenly couldn't bring myself to say it, especially to my mom.

Rather, sick is the word I'd use. "My mom is sick," I told a guy on our a second date. I figured that cancer, like anal sex, wasn't appropriate to bring up until the eighth or ninth date, when things got a little more serious.

Fortunately, I didn't have to do any of the talking. With a background in nursing, Julie had a rational and scientific explanation already prepared when the phone rang. In fact, having already practiced on Michael, her spiel was immaculate. Hearing her talk felt surreal, like a cancer Q&A. Just before we hung up, she gave me a list of book recommendations to explain more about cancer.

Julie's reaction to big events has always been to buy a book. When Brian came out of the closet, she purchased So You Have a Gay Son. Then she went through menopause and bought more books, fashioning her bedroom into her very own library. I'd walk in to see her hidden beneath stacks and stacks of books, and be bombarded with an unprovoked lesson on the changes of a mature woman's body. She became obsessed with talking about it. Sadly, now I know more about menopause than I ever imagined. Come age fifty, I'll be ready.

Unlike Julie, my go-to reaction has always been crying. More than just in times of sadness, crying is how I express all of my emotions—happiness, fear, anger, or being overwhelmed. While some people may have the ability to differentiate their cries, mine always manage to make me sound like a Wookiee at a wax parlor.

As much as I wanted to cry, it didn't make sense when my mom was able to keep so collected, talking about shopping for second opinions like it was a new car. Even though Julie has always been a calm person, part of me debated whether she was in shock. I was.

Looking for someone to confide in, I told the news to my cousin, who told my aunt, who in turn, told my birth mom. This I assume, as a few days later on the phone, she demanded to know, "Does Julie have cancer?"

I told her yes, and she grunted. It must be hard for her, I thought. Hating someone can be tricky when you find out they're sick or possibly dying. It's far easier to understand people in a cartoon sense where those who are bad are always bad and those who are good prevail. Then again, even mortal enemies like the sheep dog and the coyote clock out at the end of the day and find a way to put their differences aside while walking home together. I waited, but she didn't pry for more information, nor offer well-wishes or condolences.

After Julie started receiving treatment I asked her, "So, any weird side affects?"

"Oh my god, I can't stop eating chicken pot pies," she replied, and I smiled, picturing this listed as a possible side effect on WebMD. Wouldn't that be a field day for hypochondriacs? Teasing, I asked, "Are you sure you have cancer? Because it sounds like you're pregnant."

Rather than laugh, she said, "Don't be ridiculous. I'm going through menopause, remember?"

While Julie felt comfortable talking about her cancer, my father was not. We'd call the house inquiring for updates and if my father picked up, he'd hand the phone directly to Julie. Though he never explicitly said he didn't want to talk about her cancer, we all knew. Thus, he was the one we all worried about, not my brothers who had lost their mom, and not our mom, who actually had cancer.

To help her keep track of all her radiation appointments, Julie would write them down in a planner, and looking inside, I noticed next to every session was a sticker. Similar to the ones teachers hand out to first-graders, brightly colored stars were adorned with motivational phrases like way to go or good job!

"What are these?" I asked and she told me she wanted to monitor how she felt after each appointment.

"See, here on the twentieth I felt 'Dyn-a-mite!'" she replied earnestly. Chuckling, I kissed her forehead and told her she was brilliant.

It's not uncommon for people who have a near-death experience to get spiritual or reconnect with God. Shortly after her diagnosis, Julie started going regularly to the mall. There we bought matching faux jade elephants from a small cart vendor, who assured us the amulets brought health and happiness. She hung hers around her bedpost and so did I.

Not long after, I went to Spain to visit a friend and found myself in the town of Avila where I saw the finger of Saint Teresa. Like my jade elephant, it's said that Franco kept the finger by his bedside as a sort of talisman. While creepy, I'll admit the prospect of seeing the five-hundred-year-old finger of a saint excited me. Franco may not have been history's most beloved dictator, but he certainly did achieve success, albeit brutally. Yet standing there in the dark, I couldn't help but feel disappointed. It looked like a piece of wood with a ring shoved on it. There was nothing scary, powerful, or particularly special about it.

Proving not all was lost, just across from the finger were sanctified rose-scented rosaries. Before leaving, my mom had asked me to buy her one. When I got back, I handed the rosary to my mom and discovered she too had done some shopping; she had bought a bracelet decorated with the Turkish evil eye of protection. You had to hand it to her; she was thorough.

Seven months later, the doctor called, delivering Julie a clean bill of health. Though I can't be sure, my guess is on the elephant.

"How are you feeling?" I asked her later and she replied, "Tired. I have no strength to clean the house."

Amused, I shook my head, thinking of course you'd think that. Julie saw cancer similar to the way one thinks of a blackout, as just another one of life's random inconveniences. She made it look so easy and so, the summer after she survived breast cancer, with a mouth full of bagel, I asked her, "How do you do it?"

Without asking me to explain what I meant, she answered calmly, "I just do my best to keep moving forward and focus on the positive. That's all I can do." That was it. Then she took a bite of her half of the bagel and smiled at me. Of course it was that simple. If only practicing this philosophy were.

When the cancer came back almost two years later, this time attached to her uterus, I was living an ocean away, in Spain. Now having cancer for the second time, I waited for Julie to react and she finally did. She was annoyed.

The day before I moved to Spain, she was fired from her job where she'd worked for ten years. Unable to find steady work, she suddenly found herself collecting unemployment, avidly searching for jobs, and to her dismay, going to doctor's appointments to treat her cancer. "I know, cancer is so annoying, right?" I teased.

This time, the cancer required removal, a hysterectomy. As a woman, the thought made me squirm. Just as a kidney stone can be seen as the male equivalent to giving birth, a hysterectomy felt like the female equivalent to mental castration. Physically, I knew my mother was strong enough to endure the surgery. What scared me were the possible psychological ramifications. I didn't want my mom to see herself as less of a woman. My mom has always been resilient, but even she had to have her limits. Fearing she could have side effects even more drastic than chicken pot pies, I took a page from my mom's book and read up on it.

Using the Internet as a medical reference is not something I generally do or advise others to do. I know far too many people who have incorrectly self-diagnosed themselves or worse, scared themselves into thinking they have cancer. Should a friend tell me they read a web article and subsequently suspect they're a celiac, I'll remind them there's a reason medical students go to school for seven years, and that if just anyone could do it, we'd all have a medical degree from Google University.

Forgetting my objections, I looked up hysterectomy and immediately wished I had taken my own advice. There, listed under side effects were drastic mood change and depression, due to the change in hormone levels.

For those who have not personally experienced the irrational craze that can come with a surge or drop in hormones, I can only describe it as a tsunami. You know this destructive force is coming, but you're powerless to stop it. All you can do is tell people to flee to safety until it's passed. Though Julie is strong, the possibility of losing her not just to cancer, but to hormones, terrified me.

The surgery took place around Thanksgiving and left Julie with several stitches in her abdomen, making it uncomfortable to laugh, as she told me over Skype. Nevertheless, she giggled every time my niece performed her latest trick, which involved hiding an object underneath the corner of our dining room rug, pretending it had disappeared. Though my niece couldn't really talk, her face and hands managed to say, where'd it go? Then, once convinced she'd successfully tricked her audience, she'd unveil the object and squeal with delight. Ta-da! Only a year old, this was enough to entertain her for hours, and so everything within reach was grabbed and placed under the rug, again and again. Despite her pain, Julie laughed each time, smiling proudly at her granddaughter.

Watching my mother smile at the simple joy of my niece's trick eased whatever fear previously I had. Cancer wasn't going to change Julie. Uterus or no uterus, my mom would always be strong. For in fact, cancer was like the five-hundred-year-old finger of St Teresa. Neither had any real power, except for the power that people gave it.

the way

The city where I was assigned to teach in Spain is a small holy city called Santiago de Compostela, located in the autonomous community of Galicia. Similar to the rest of Spain, its economy is based on tourism. Every year, tens of thousands of people from all around the world make a pilgrimage that involves walking hundreds of miles to the cathedral in Santiago. The pilgrimage, called *el camino* or *the way* in English, is meant to be a sort of spiritual journey. Though there are many ways one can come to Santiago, I ended up there by chance.

Galicia was not my first choice when applying to my program, nor was it my second or third. In fact, it wasn't on my list at all because when I applied, Galicia wasn't an option. My first choice had been Madrid. However, the selection process for my program was first-come, first-served, and I had applied at the last minute, thanks to Gums.

He and I had gotten back together late that winter, and figuring I'd move to L.A. once the school year was over, I put off applying. Then in March when I mentioned the subject again he said, "Oh, you were serious about that? I thought you were going to Spain." I told him I was, and ended it.

With a day to spare, I got my application in and was wait-listed. There I would have stayed, had Galicia not decided in mid-summer that it was going to participate in the program. As a result, I was assigned to Galicia, a place no one had ever heard of.

After looking it up, I asked my roommate in Brooklyn, Becky, who had spent two years in Barcelona teaching English, if she'd ever heard of Galicia. "Sure. My roommate in Barcelona was from Galicia," Becky told me. "Sweet girl, but I remember she would always talk about how the women from Galicia were known for being curt, you know, the no-nonsense type." Based on her tone, I couldn't tell if this was a good or bad thing. Well, they can't be worse than New Yorkers, I told myself optimistically. I can live with that.

Then I mentioned Galicia to another friend. "Ohhh…I've been there," she said, rather ominously. "Twenty years ago when I was about your age. Yeah, it's in the middle of nowhere. Back then it was just a poor small fishing community. I can't imagine it's changed much. The people there are all about tradition. I mean, really." Great, I thought. Then she added, "You know, it's not like the rest of Spain, it's very cold and rainy. You're going to want to pack a lot of thermal underwear." Right, even better.

the way

That September I arrived to Santiago and stayed at a small youth hostel situated on the outskirts of town. Though the hostel's location wasn't ideal, it was clean and offered free Wifi and breakfast. There I met a young Belgian man named Shane, who, as he explained to me over breakfast the next morning, was attempting to hitchhike his way across the world. Of course you are, I thought to myself, eyeing his Birkenstocks and long ponytail. He looked like a guy you'd see playing hacky sack on Haight Street. However, not wanting to be completely rude, I granted him a skeptical, "Uh huh," and continued to groggily butter my toast.

Despite my general bubbly appearance, I'm not much of a morning person or one to talk to strangers. In fact, when traveling on planes I'll usually pretend to be asleep when my seatmate arrives, just in case they're the talkative type. Yet right when I was about to politely ignore him, he said something that caught my attention.

Apparently, the night before he met an older, middle-aged woman in a park. He went home with her, led to believe by their ten-minute conversation in broken Spanish that she ran a boarding house for students. Intrigued, I listened as he explained that by house, the woman had meant a small one-bedroom second-floor apartment. Since the woman had forgotten her keys inside, they had to enter through the window using a ladder.

Once inside, the woman, or sea cow as he called her, stripped off her clothes and kindly offered to share her only bed with Shane. When he gently refused, instead taking a place on the floor, she got up and sat on the chair beside him, where she proceeded to talk until the break of dawn, which is when he made his escape. "So that's how I almost got raped by a sea cow," he concluded.

It's true what they say; one of the most interesting things about moving abroad is the people you meet. However, before moving to Spain I imagined that these people would be like Shane, foreign travelers with fascinating stories or better yet, Spanish people. I did not come to Spain to meet more Americans, I thought. I was going to immerse myself in the Spanish culture. Become Spanish, if I could.

Accordingly, when I met Rachel, a college student from New York studying abroad, I gave her the same tepid reception I had Shane. While I didn't go out of my way to be nice to Rachel, I didn't go out of my way to be ungracious either. After all, she was my roommate at the hostel and I didn't want to make things unpleasant. Plus, she was undeniably warm and funny, making it all the more difficult to be aloof. I don't care how nice she is, we are not going to be friends. This is what I told myself the first day. By the second day, we were out to lunch. What was I supposed to do, decline her offer? Tell her, "Thank you, but I was just kidding a second ago when I said I was hungry and going to get food?" Of course not. So I went, and as predicted, had a lovely time.

At lunch I learned that like me, Rachel was mixed. Half white and half Mexican, she had amazing green eyes and dark olive skin. Yet more than stunning, Rachel was smart and a foodie. Other than the fact that she didn't drink coffee, there really wasn't a single thing I didn't like about her. Fine, you're allowed one American buddy, I told myself as we left the cafe.

Then Laura came, another American assigned to Galicia through my program. What first stuck me about Laura was her beauty. She looked exotic, as if she could be from anywhere, though in reality she was from California and fit the stereotype: ultra liberal, crunchy, and an actress. While beauty like Laura's can sometimes be intimidating, her sweet and open personality made her all the more personable. Right after dropping her stuff off in our room and a quick introduction, she told Rachel and I, "I'm going to go down to the garden and play my fiddle barefoot, so I can connect with the Earth."

"I like her," Rachel declared, after Laura had left the room. Nodding my head, I agreed.

And then there were three.

I met Aaron on my fourth day in town. He was a classmate of Rachel's back in New York and was also staying at the hostel. Prior to coming to Spain, Aaron worked as a bike messenger in the city. Consequently, he had absolutely no body fat and the physique of a pubescent boy, which his anxious personality only exaggerated.

Whereas Rachel had an easy grace to her, Aaron was one of those people who had no couth. One of my favorite stories is the time Rachel mentioned to Aaron that she wasn't feeling well. Usually, when most people hear a statement such as this, the standard reply is something along the lines of, "Aww, what's wrong?" However, Aaron, not being like most people said, "Yeah, I've noticed you've put on a little weight."

"What? Why would you say that?"

"Well, you said you weren't feeling well and I thought, well, what's a reason people don't feel well? Because they've gained weight. You've gained weight and so I thought you were asking me if I thought you had, and you have."

To be fair, Aaron had redeeming qualities. At times, he could be sweet and compassionate, and some would even say insightful. I remember telling him that spring, "Alex is a douchebag!"

"Wait, what exactly is a douchebag and how do I avoid being one?" Aaron asked.

"It means he thinks his shit doesn't stink!" I clarified.

"Well, that's physically impossible," he explained. "When you eat a lot of vegetables you have more active bacteria in your digestive tract. When my roommate poops, which is once a week, the whole apartment smells." Then, I think, as a way to console me, he added, "You know, my father once told me that people highly overestimate the value of good sex and underestimate the value of a good shit."

"I think your father was just trying to keep you out of trouble in high school," I told him, not wanting to admit that Aaron had just made me realize something profound. But Aaron was surprising like that, which is why we kept him around. Besides, it wasn't like any of us were any less eccentric.

Brian showed up to the hostel a day after Aaron. He too was in my program and like Aaron, had his idiosyncrasies. However, Brian was good-looking and knew it, which gave him the confidence and leeway to get away with things that other people normally couldn't. For instance, his dancing was empirically bad. Really he only had one move, which involved a robotic interpretation of the bees' knees. Not surprisingly, we walked into a club one night to find Brian and all of his Brazilian roommates doing The Brian.

While I hadn't intended on making any American friends, I knew that these people were a group of individuals I'd regret not knowing. Thus in spite of myself, I found myself surrounded by Americans in Spain.

Nevertheless, I continued to try to assimilate into the Spanish culture. Outside of my co-workers, all married and on the verge of retirement, I found it difficult to meet many people from Spain, however. Though friendly, the Spanish have an insular culture. Most have lived their entire lives within one hundred kilometers of where they were born and as a result, have had the same friends their whole lives. Were I to meet one who suddenly wanted a new friend, what would I have said?

The very reason I had a job was because the Spanish are admittedly terrible at English. My Spanish-speaking capabilities were limited to ordering coffee or other things found in traveling guidebooks. It's not that I didn't want to learn Spanish but rather, that I lacked the proper motivation one needs to learn another language. Specifically, a boyfriend. Anyone will tell you that the best way to learn a language is to get a lover. Despite my efforts, nothing seemed to work out.

Late that December, the Sailor and I decided to stop seeing each other. We had been dating for only six months and truthfully, when it ended I wasn't so much surprised as I was saddened. We were friends going in, and friends going out. As a result, for the first time in years, I was single and without any sort of romantic entanglement.

This is a good thing, I told myself for the first month. However, it didn't take long before I started feeling lonely. And while Santiago is filled with many eligible bachelors, none were interested in me, an Asian-looking American girl with a grown-out Justin Bieber haircut. Unfortunately, the only guys who'd hit on me were creeps with girlfriends, like Franz, who stood in the plaza outside my window screaming my name at three o'clock in the morning. "Alison! Put on your pee-yamas! I need to see you!" Perhaps not my finest moment, but I'd wager to say it wasn't his, either.

My drunken Romeo was Karin's fault. Karin was a friend I'd met through Rachel. She gave Franz my number and told him where I lived after running into him at the club later that night. "I thought you liked him," she explained. "I didn't know you left because you found out he had a girlfriend. He sounded so sincere when I talked to him and said it was all a misunderstanding. I asked him if he had a girlfriend and he promised me he didn't."

"Never believe what a guy tells you when drunk at three o'clock in the morning," I told Karin, as we sat curled up on the couch in my living room.

My first apartment in Santiago was like a horror story you read about on Craigslist. For one, the bathroom was small and unventilated, so two weeks after moving in, black and green mold started to form on the ceiling. Still, this was nothing in comparison to the shower, which came equipped with its own obstacle course. To take a shower one had to stand sideways in order to avoid knocking into the ceramic soap shelf, which hung by a single bolt, despite the large crack in the wall. Then there was the time the bathroom light bulb spontaneously exploded as I was showering, which is how I ended up standing in the dark surrounded by millions of tiny glass shards, with nothing but shampoo on my head. Sadly, I spent a fair amount of my first year in Spain cooped up that bathroom, but not for reasons that you'd imagine.

Our landlord hadn't bothered to mention it, but the apartment was too old to install a phone line or Internet. After various failed attempts to get Internet, my roommate and I resorted to going door to door, asking for Internet as if it were a cup of sugar. Luckily, we were able to convince our next-door neighbor to share her Wi-Fi at a modest price. The only drawback was that the signal was too weak to reach my room. Thus, if I wanted to use the Internet at home, I had to sit on the toilet. Sounds awful, yet this was one of the nicer apartments Kathrin and I saw while searching for places together. And though the apartment was undoubtedly a piece of shit, it was our piece of shit, and we loved it.

My roommate Kathrin and I met through work. She was from Munich and was assigned to be the German conversation teacher at my school. While Kathrin was sweet and polite, initially we hadn't planned on living together. Both of us wanted to find Spanish roommates in order to improve our Spanish. This turned out to be more difficult than we expected.

The way one looks for an apartment in Spain is by going from lamppost to lamppost, taking down numbers from tiny roommate ads, which conveniently have no dates on them. Differentiating whether a post is a week, month, or year old, is virtually impossible. Just to be safe, I wrote them all down.

Then with my limited Spanish, I attempted to call these numbers. Yet more often than not, I'd learn that the room was already rented or that I couldn't understand the person. On the rare occasion that I could understand the person I was speaking with, I'd discover that the apartment was in disrepair or involved living with a fifty-year-old hermit and his five cats. Consequently, I left each apartment similar to the same way one ends a bad first date, with, "So I'll call you." This is how I spent my first week in Spain, acquainting myself with lampposts.

When I met up with Kathrin a few days later, she admitted to encountering similar difficulties. Disillusioned with our quest to live with a native Spanish speaker, we agreed to find an apartment together, but this time, with the help of a broker. Thus, by default, Kathrin and I ended up as roommates.

Kathrin turned out to be an ideal roommate. She was quiet, clean and responsible. When it came to making decisions, I found that we agreed on most things, such as what to buy for the apartment, since our furnished apartment was not so furnished after all. At first, we only bought what was necessary: four cups, four plates, two bowls, a handful of utensils and a drying rack for our clothes. Bigger, fancier purchases such as a blender, we rationalized, weren't worth buying. Our lease would end in June, in not even a year. In the meantime, we'd content ourselves with living simply. And that we did.

a beautiful mess

That June came faster than I would have liked. For in June, my program finished, the university went on break, and all of my friends returned home. I was the only one in our group of friends who had decided to stay, not that everyone necessarily had a choice. "Are you sure you want to finish up college?" I asked Karin, "It's really overrated. I assure you."

I wasn't ready for it to be over. I was comforted by the thought that everything in life comes to an end. But while taking the LSATs, the idea of it pertaining to my precious life in Santiago was devastating. I loved our weekly potlucks, outdoor yoga sessions, and drinks at our local bar.

With each goodbye, I couldn't help but feel like I was six years old again, begging my mom, "Please, just five more minutes," back when I thought five minutes was a lifetime. Suddenly, I questioned whether renewing my contract for another year in Spain had been the right decision.

Staying would mean having to start over yet again. I'd have to find a new apartment, new roommates, and new friends, except this time in Spanish. Part of me dreaded staying just to avoid the humiliation. One can only use the excuse "I just moved here" for so long before people suspect that you're lazy or worse, dimwitted. This would be my second time around. Things were supposed to get easier. Yet everything felt just as difficult as the first time, if not more without my support network.

Still, leaving Santiago didn't feel right either. I may not have made many Spanish friends or learned much Spanish, but in many ways Santiago felt like home. After years of bouncing around from city to city, Santiago was the first place that made me want to stand still. While coming to Santiago didn't fix my problems, I no longer felt hindered by my failed relationships. Just like the pilgrims who traveled on foot for days, I looked onto the cathedral from the window in the school where I taught, and knew I had arrived.

Nothing may have gone as planned my first year in Spain, but it was still one of the best years of my life. Perhaps that's why, despite knowing there was no guarantee that things in Santiago were going to work out, I decided to stay. Maybe it wouldn't last, but what does?

a map of my mess

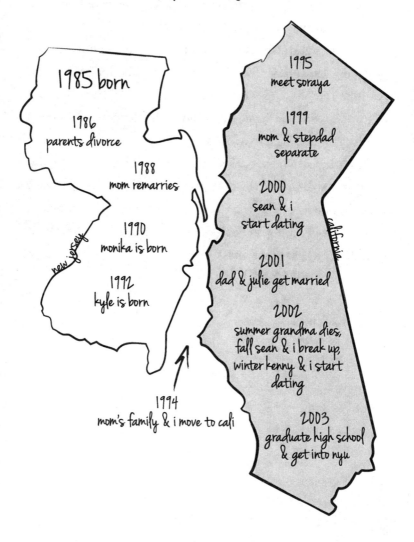

2004
kenny & i break up

2005
jan. kenny dies,
aug. monika gets sick
& sean & i date again

2008
election day,
gums & i
break up

new york

2006
dec. sean & i break
up for good, the
muslim ra & i start
dating & break up

2007
mar. gums &
i start dating,
i begin teaching
& grad school

2009
my mom, julie,
gets diagnosed
with cancer,
six months later
she beats it

2010
aug. my mom & i break up,
sept. i quit my job & move to spain

2010
start teaching, mom gets
diagnosed with cancer again,
i write a book & despite everything,
i have the best year of my life

2011
feb. my mom beats cancer again,
i twist my ankle & decide
to stay in spain

spain

present

213

about the author

Ali Berlinski was born in New Jersey but considers herself bicoastal as half her childhood was spent in Northern California after her parent's divorce. She attended NYU, majored in Sociology, graduated cum laude and earned a dual masters in Education from CUNY Brooklyn College. She then joined the NYC Teaching Fellows program and taught special education in Brooklyn, New York.

Currently, Ali Berlinski lives in Northern Spain where she continues to teach and write. This is her first novel.

www.aliberlinski.com

discovered by

Amanda Barbara

Genevieve Little

William Rodriguez

Ka Ki Wong-Tin

Marcus Langston

Diego Pellitero

David Montminy

Kim Nouhan-Puzzo

Christopher Kalicki

Antonius Picter Spek

Hellen Barbara

Barton Ching

Christina Berlinski

Derek Valenzuela

Roberto Carbono

Camille Tamara Arnaiz

Mike Berlinski

Ka Ki Wong

Jesse Potash

Neil Grosscup

Nicholas Scordato

Megan Walker

Brian Berlinski

Stephen Kristan

Brian Bigornia

Brianne Glover

Tori Riley Sander

Kellie Klein

Mary Kate Moore

Danielle Aita

Kelly Donnelly

Rebecca Dow

Kathryn Minas

Danielle Levoit

Ann Seestadt

Lisa O'Gara

a beautiful mess

Roberto Berlinski

Diane Gray

Robert Gibson

Thomas Consiglio

Ann Rosenbush

Justine Schofield

Gail Aronoff

Sarah Farrell

Zachary L Mahone

Maliha Salim

Soraya Foutouhi

Levon Kendall

Deborah Shaghaghi

Caitlin Davis

Kim Nouhan-Puzzo

Telma Lago

Megan Sweeney

Serena Robinett

Javier Perez

James R Thomsen

Nidhi Jain

David G. Carriere

R. Leslie Valenzuela

Kevin Siu

CPSIA information can be obtained at www.ICGtesting.com
Printed in the USA
LVOW12s1958150713

342958LV00010B/1053/P